The Wit & Wisdom of

MUSIC

First Published in Great Britain in 2006 by
House of Raven Book Services
King's Sutton
OX17 3RS

© 2006 House of Raven

Typeset in Trixie Cameo and Unica
Design, photography and illustration: David Coventon
Additional design: Jean-Luke Epstein, Patrik Hartmann, Bradley Hotson, Tom Hutchings, Stuart Weston

Printed in China by Imago

ISBN: 1905403038

The Wit & Wisdom of MUSIC

Compiled by Nick Holt

A lot of people thought Rock and Roll would be a passing fancy. They were wrong. A lot of people think Rock and Roll will save the planet. They're wrong, too, whatever Bono might say.

It's just music. Much of it insipid and forgettable. But now and then you hear something and feel that little knot in the pit of your stomach uncurl and shake to the beat. And then it can be uplifting and, yes, a little inspiring.

Neil Young knew the score:
"Hey hey, my my. Rock and Roll will never die."

CONTENTS

There are over 1,000 quotes in this collection. Each quote that appears is numbered (i.e. •123). These numbers run sequentially throughout the book. Use the index at the back to find Rock Stars, Pop Stars, Songwriters, Musicians, and commentators contributing to this collection. The index is listed in alphabetical order by surname.

I was born in 1961.
Like so many of my generation,
I owe most of my musical
history to one man.
John Peel.

1

Let there be light… sound… drums… guitar…
Let there be Rock!!!

A.C./D.C. *Let There Be Rock* (1977),
from the album *Let There Be Rock!* •1

LET THERE BE ROCK!!!

11

All the good music has already been written by people with wigs and stuff.

Frank Zappa •2

Rock has always been the devil's music.

David Bowie circa 1988 •3

There's no bullshit going down with rock and roll. It's an honest form and one of the most open. It encompasses poetry, jazz and just about anything you can imagine... it is the highest form. It goes beyond, colour, gender, anything. Patti Smith, Cashbox, 1976 •4

Have you ever wondered why young people take to music like fish to water? Maybe it's because music is fun. Plain and simple. It opens up their minds to dream great dreams about where they can go and what they can do when they get older.

Isaac Hayes •5

You better lose yourself in the music, the moment,
You own it, you better never let it go.
You only get one shot, do not miss your chance to blow.
This opportunity comes once in a lifetime.

Eminem *Lose Yourself* (2003) from *8 Mile* OST •6

Rock and Roll is an expression of the energy of life, the energy that comes from the realization you're alive, projecting it outwards. You just wanna stamp your feet and wave your hands in the air.

Ian Astbury of The Cult 2001 •7

Rock and roll is the lowest form of life known to man.

Elvis Costello 1977 •8

It seemed such a sexy, pagan horror, such a dangerous new creature, that America feared it, preached against it, and tried to ban it.

Nick Tosches on rock 'n' roll •9

I love rock 'n' roll. I think it's an exciting art form. It's revolutionary. Still revolutionary and it changed people. It changed their hearts.

Nick Cave •10

Rock 'n' roll's supposed to take you away from the shit job you're in for an hour and a half and make you feel 100 feet tall.

Lemmy •11

Rock 'n' roll's never about giving up. For me – for a lot of kids – it was a total positive force, not optimistic all the time, but positive. It was never, never, about surrender.

Bruce Springsteen, 1981 •12

The best rock and roll music encapsulates a certain high energy – an angriness – whether on record or onstage, Rock and roll is only rock and roll if it's not safe.

Mick Jagger of The Rolling Stones circa 1981 •13

The allure of popular culture has always been its promise of a walk on the wild side.

Cosmo Landesman •14

Chain reaction running through my veins
Pumps the bass line up into my brain
Screws my mind until I lose control
And when the building rocks I know it's got my soul.

Girls Aloud, *Sound of the Underground,* (2003), from the album *Sound of the Underground* •15

When you listen to good rock and roll you wanna feel fucking dirty afterwards. You should feel so dirty you have to take a shower. Rock and roll should be like pornography... The filthier the better.

Frank Black 1996 •16

Rock 'n' roll is like a drug.
I don't take very much, but when I do
rock 'n' roll, I fuckin' do it.
But I don't want to do it all at the
time 'cause it'll kill me.

Neil Young 1988 •17

I never thought of rock and roll as this big cultural thing
and worried about the state of it and all. It's like, plug that
fucking guitar in and give me a backseat, and 'it' lives.

Paul Westerberg ex-The Replacements 1993 •18

Rock and roll is about attitude.
I couldn't care less about technique.

Johnny Thunders 1977 •19

I don't know anything
about music. I've done
it all through acting.

Rock star Meatloaf reveals the secret of his success •20

One chord is fine,
Two chords are pushing it,
Three chords and you're into jazz.

Lou Reed circa 1975 •21

It just bores me because it's too easy.
Anyone can be that complicated.
Three notes is far cleverer than three hundred if
they're arranged in the right way, and that's what
pop music is all about.

Brett Anderson disses classical music, 1994 •22

No matter what direction rock goes in,
it has to stay with the blues. That's
the spine and body of it.

Eric Clapton •23

You're a blues person only when you're playing.
But Negro blues men live the blues environment,
eat soul food. Even hearing them talk can be like
hearing the blues. Rock is like a battery that must
always go back to blues to get recharged.

Eric Clapton 1968 •24

I can't play long solos anymore without boring myself.

Eric Clapton 2001 •25

Calling out around the world
Are you ready for a brand new beat?
Summer's here and the time is right
For dancing in the street.

Martha Reeves and the Vandellas *Dancing In The Street*,
(Mickey Stevenson & Marvin Gaye) (1964) •26

**Most people get into bands for three
very simple rock and roll reasons:
to get laid, to get fame and to get rich.**

Bob Geldof, *Melody Maker*, 1977 •27

**The whole rock 'n' roll lifestyle?
Well, basically, we never had one.**

Margo Timmins of Cowboy Junkies •28

We want to be phalluses ramming in the butthole of pop.

Gibby Haynes of The Butthole Surfers 1993 •29

A rock 'n' roll group is a banding together of individuals for the purpose of achieving something that none of them can get on their own: money, fame, the right sound, something less easy to put into words.

Greil Marcus •30

Music for the neck downwards.

Keith Richards on rock 'n' roll •31

If you look at the history of innovation in music, it all happens by accident. Innovative music has never come, from my perspective, from a bunch of academics sitting around.

Moby 2001 •32

Spector, while still in his teens, seemed to comprehend the prole vitality of rock 'n' roll that has made it the kind of darling holy beast of intellectuals in the United States, England, and France.

Tom Wolfe *The First Tycoon of Teen,* 1965 •33

The mistake which most critics make is to persist in trying to evaluate pop culture as if it were something else: the equivalent of insisting on considering a bicycle as if it were a horse. George Melly *Revolt Into Style* (1970) •34

Rock 'n' Roll is about music.
Music. Music. Music.
It's not about you,
it's not about me,
it's not about Oasis.
It's about the songs.

Noel Gallagher, 1994 •35

Rock 'n' roll is not just music. You're selling an attitude, too. Take away the attitude and you're just like anyone else. The kids need a sense of adventure and rock 'n' roll gives it to them. Wham out the hardest and cruellest lyrics as propaganda, speak the truth as clearly as possible.

Malcolm McLaren •36

Younger musicians than The Sex Pistols and their peers, the provincial ex-punks who were to start the Ska revival of the late 1970s, would carry this golden rule with them into the future. The first law of punk was – you can do it. Play an instrument – you can do it. Form a band – you can do it. Go onstage – what's stopping you?

Tony Parsons in *Bare* magazine in 1988 •37

When a folk club artist goes out with his guitar, he might think he's James Taylor or Bob Dylan. I still think I'm The Clash.

Billy Bragg •38

A rock and roll band needs four instruments. That's a fucking fact not an opinion. As for The White Stripes, that's not rock and roll, that's performance art.

Steve Van Zandt, 2006 •39

There's always going to be the bands who change the way the river flows, and there are always going to be people who get in their boats and ride down afterwards.

Billy Corgan of Smashing Pumpkins, 1993 •40

We're like bad architecture or an old whore. If you stick around long enough, eventually you get respectable.

Jerry Garcia paraphrasing a quote from the movie, *Chinatown* •41

I do think rock 'n' roll should be glamorous and beautiful and sexy.

Tanya Donnelly of Belly, 1995 •42

Nothing is as important as passion. No matter what you want to do with your life, be passionate.

Jon Bon Jovi •43

Music is madness. It's like a beautiful curse. When you and me are dead, man, it will still go on, which is beautiful.

Paul Weller gets all misty-eyed, March 2006 •44

2

**Nothing's gonna
touch you in these
Golden years**

David Bowie
Golden Years (1976) •45

GOLDEN

YEARS

**All music is folk music, I ain't
ever heard no horse sing a song.**

Louis Armstrong quoted in the *New York Times* •46

**Pop music prior to the early 60s had been
purely about escapism. Escaping from the
rigours of having a humdrum life, from living
in a post-war society, from all those things.**

Pete Townshend •47

**I made *Bo Diddley* in '55, they
started playing it, and everybody
freaked out. Caucasian kids threw
Beethoven into the garbage can.**

Bo Diddley •48

**I opened the door for a lot of people and they
just ran through, and left me holding the knob.**

Bo Diddley •49

Buddy Holly was the gentleman of rockabilly, the first soft rocker.

Nick Tosches •50

Either be hot or cold. If you are lukewarm, the Lord will spew you forth from His mouth.

Jerry Lee Lewis •51

I can't stand to sing the same song the same way two nights in succession, let alone two years or ten years. If you can, then it ain't music, it's close-order drill or exercise or yodelling or something, not music.

Billie Holiday *Lady Sings The Blues* (1956) •52

My ambition was to eat. We were very hungry.

James Brown on his childhood •53

Brown develops a number through a series of crescendos – mounting steadily in volume, fervour and drive – until the rising tension demands the release of shouting and body movement. The physical side of love has seldom been projected with such excitement and power as Brown can command.

Arnold Shaw 1969 •54

None of the new generation can ever be the Godfather. The only people that qualify are myself and Sinatra. It's God's business that nobody can fill my shoes.

James Brown 1988 •55

This was my richest time, with all my hit records selling all over the country and me and my band working every night. The river was running. The river of loot.

Little Richard •56

Smokey is lovely. He sings lead in the perfect woman's soprano, not a falsetto shriek or anything so vulgar, but a finely controlled warble, full of its own small subtleties. Pop's first female impersonator, original prima donna.

Nik Cohn on Smokey Robinson •57

Every time you hear his voice on the radio, you feel that they're playing music again.

Bobby Womack on Smokey Robinson •58

In person, everything he does is an all out, powerhouse, total emotional explosion. He may start singing *Try a Little Tenderness* with tenderness, but it always ends up 'sock it to me, baby...' he can work listeners into a frenzy more quickly than any nightclub performer of his time. Ralph J. Gleason on Otis Redding •59

Modulation, shading, dynamics, progression, emotion. Every essential quality – he had it all.

Jerry Wexler on Sam Cooke •60

You had to crossover – get the white business as well as the black business.

Curtis Mayfield •61

In the manner of the very greatest rock 'n' roll, Sly and the Family Stone made music no one had ever heard before.

Greil Marcus •62

Curtis Mayfield, for me, is an encyclopaedia. Every time I listen to his songs they never seem to age, and they always seem appropriate for whatever else is going on in society.

Jazzie B on the influential Curtis Mayfield •63

There's nobody in the world can make better records than I do.

Phil Spector •64

In the 1960s they all treated us like we were great philosopher gods that knew all the answers...

Paul Kantner of Jefferson Airplane •65

We were inspiring each other. I miss [the 1960's] quite a bit. I think about how great music was then and how inspired everybody was. It seems like it's all gone away. People aren't making very many records these days.

Brian Wilson of The Beach Boys, 2001 •66

Never was it easier to gain a reputation as a seer, never was a following so rapidly and readily acquired.

Bernard Levin on the Sixties,
The Pendulum Years, 1970 •67

Skiffle was the start of British rock music. It was all about feel rather than content. It had style.

Lonnie Donegan •68

I strode onstage wearing an eye patch after being struck in the eye by a guitar string – and never looked back.

Johnny Kidd of Johnny Kidd and the Pirates •69

I'm not being big headed, but The Kinks were unique – it's like getting to the North Pole first. Really, until we started diversifying, we couldn't be touched.

The modest Ray Davies •70

When Lou and I started the group, there was a basic understanding: it seemed more important to be different than immediately successful, to have a personality of our own, to have arrangements like *Venus In Furs* and to give concerts that were never the same.

John Cale on the Velvet Underground •71

I won't retire until the people retire me.

B.B. King •72

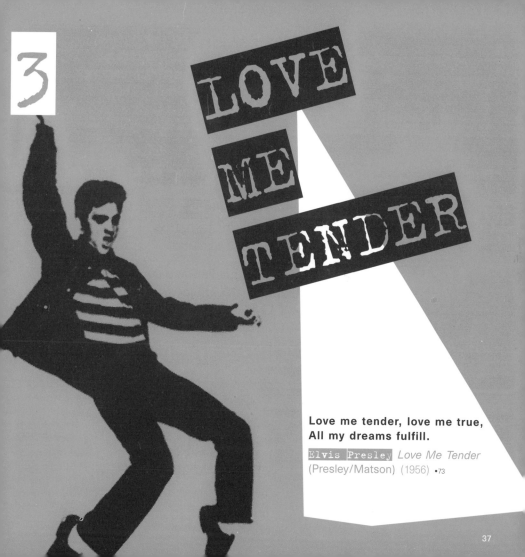

3

LOVE ME TENDER

**Love me tender, love me true,
All my dreams fulfill.**

Elvis Presley *Love Me Tender*
(Presley/Matson) (1956) •73

What rock needed to get it off the ground was a universal hero, a symbol, a rallying point... obviously, Bill Haley didn't measure up. Equally obviously, Elvis Presley did...

Nik Cohn in *Awopbopaloobop,* 1968 •74

The reason I taped Elvis was this: over and over I remember Sam saying, if only I could find a white man who had the Negro feel, I could make a billion dollars. This is what I heard in Elvis, this... what I guess they now call soul, this Negro sound.

Marion Keisher who made the first taped recording of Elvis •75

This was the major teen breakthrough and Elvis triggered it. In this way, without even trying, he became one of the people who have radically affected the way that people think and live.

Nik Cohn •76

The teddy boys were waiting for Elvis Presley. Everybody under 20 all over the world was waiting.

Jeff Nuttall in *Bomb Culture,* 1968 •77

This was punk rock.
This was revolt.
It's all there in that
elastic voice and body.

Bono on Elvis •78

If the police had not been there, forming a blue wall on the stage, the audience might have eaten Elvis's body in a Eucharistic frenzy. They were his and he was theirs, the leader: it was the incandescent moment.

Stanley Booth on Elvis' famous Memphis charity concert in 1956 •79

The story of Heartbreak Hotel is this: Mae Boren Axton, songwriter and Hank Snow's PR lady, was shown a newspaper clipping by her friend Tommy Durden, another songwriter. The clipping reported a suicide by a young man who left a one line note, 'I walk a lonely street'. Axton and Durden wrote the song around the line and made a tape of it within half an hour.

Nick Tosches •80

Blue Suede Shoes was even more to the point. This had been a hit for Carl Perkins in 1956 as Elvis took it over the following year and give it wholly new dimensions. It was important – the idea that clothes could dominate your life.

Nik Cohn 1968 •81

When I first met Elvis, he had a million dollars worth of talent. Now he has a million dollars.

Colonel Tom Parker •82

I don't aim to let this fame business get me. God gave me a voice. If I turned against God, I'd be finished.

Elvis Presley quoted by Tony Palmer, 1976 •83

The kind of stardom that was visited on Elvis Presley was simply more than he could handle.

Charles Shaar Murray No shit, Sherlock •84

Elvis is the dream gone wrong, that's why as a character he's so fascinating. His demise was such a public one. He was for a lot of people the definition of America, all its promise, all it could achieve and all the freedom of the country.

The Edge •85

The awful spectacle of a great star, falling apart among servants and minders, shocked Elton to the core. Philip Norman on Elton John's meeting with Elvis in 1976 •86

Elvis Presley is a supreme figure in American life, one whose presence, no matter how banal or predictable, brooks no real comparisons.

Greil Marcus in Mystery Train, 1977 •87

His violent hip-swinging during an obvious attempt to copy Elvis Presley was revolting. Hardly the kind of performance any parent could wish their child to witness.

NME in 1958 on that notorious rebel, Cliff Richard •88

Elvis Presley recorded a song of mine...
that's the one recording I treasure the most...
it was called *Tomorrow Is A Long Time*.

Bob Dylan •89

I'm a really big Elvis fan and I think the reason
why we did the whole Elvis thing is because
you know, he's from Vegas.

Britney Spears •90

The book is a prodigy of bad writing,
excitable, sarcastic and only fleetingly
literate. It is also as exploitative as the
exploiters whom Goldman reviles, and
no more tasteful than an Elvis jumpsuit.

Martin Amis on Albert Goldman's *Elvis* •91

Mini tycoon Jonathan King, radiantly happy to be in
front of the cameras even on such a solemn occasion,
said that this was a doubly important death because
the man doing the dying had been entirely created by the
media. Tony Palmer said it would be a pity to leave the
audience with the impression that anyone as talented as
Elvis Presley had been entirely created by the media.
Jonathan King said, 'I agree with Tony Palmer'.

Clive James in *The Observer*, on a TV tribute to Elvis •92

I tell you,
Elvis can't last.

Jackie Gleason 1956 •93

**Elvis is where pop begins and ends.
He's the great original and, even now,
he's the image that makes all others
seem shoddy; the boss. For once,
the fan club's spiel is justified:
Elvis is King.**

Nik Cohn •94

**If life was fair, Elvis would be alive
and all the impersonators would be dead.**

Johnny Carson *The Tonight Show,* NBC TV •95

There have been contenders. There have been pretenders. But there is still only one King – Elvis Presley.

Bruce Springsteen 1975 •96

HEROES

4

I, I will be King
And you, you will be Queen.
Though nothing will drive them away,
We can be heroes
Just for one day.

David Bowie *"Heroes"* (1977)
from the album *"Heroes"* •97

Louis Jordan's *Saturday Night Fish Fry* is the perfect record. Somewhere between jump, jazz and R&B, it is a whole way of life in one song – it shows that rock and roll did not start with Bill Haley.

Jerry Dammers of The Specials •98

My music made your liver quiver, your bladder spatter, your knees freeze. And your big toe shoot right up in your boot.

Little Richard •99

He'd scream and scream and scream. He had a freak voice, tireless, hysterical, completely indestructible, and he never in his life sang at anything lower than an enraged bull like roar. On every phrase, he'd embroider with squeals, rasps, siren whoops. His stamina, his drive were limitless.

Nik Cohn on Little Richard •100

You knew not, night to night, where he was going to come from. He just burst onto the stage from anywhere. You wouldn't be able to hear anything but the roar of the audience. He might come out and walk on the piano. He might go out into the audience. His charisma was just a whole new thing to the business. Richard was totally out of this world, wild, and it gave people who wanted to scream a chance to go ahead and scream instead of trying to be cool.

H.B.Barnum Richard's sax player •101

As a person he was brash, fast, bombastic, a sort of prototype Muhammad Ali.

Nik Cohn on Little Richard •102

He drove the whole house into a complete frenzy. There is no single phrase to describe his hold on the audience. It might excite some and terrify others. It's hypnotic, like an evangelistic meeting where, for want of a better phrase, Richard is the disciple and the audience the flock that follows. I couldn't believe the power of Little Richard on stage. He was amazing.

Mick Jagger •103

Jerry Lee learned how to rock 'n' roll from me. He was just a country singer till he heard my songs and he recorded a lot of them.

Little Richard on his influence on Jerry Lee Lewis •104

Richard taught Hendrix a lot of things, and Hendrix got a lot of things from Richard. That's where he got the charisma. Richard used to say, look, don't be ashamed to do whatever you feel. Marquette Little Richard's road manager •105

They asked me to come back the next day and I said if they gave me ten bob I would. So they gave me the ten bob and I came back.

Noël Redding on joining Jimi Hendrix' band •106

James Brown and Frank Sinatra are two different quantities in the universe. They represent two different experiences of the world.

Amiri Baraka poet and activist, in an interview with David Frost 1970 •107

If you're talking about really heavy people – heavy, heavy, heavy – I'd say Burt Bacharach.

James Brown •108

Michael Jackson, he used to watch my from the wings and got his moon walk from my camel walk. I ain't jealous, I'm zealous. I ain't teased, I'm pleased.

James Brown •109

I've always loved Steve Winwood. I used to go and see the Spencer Davis Group when I was 18 and he was about 16. He used to play really great guitar as well as great piano – I wanted to hit the little fucker, he was so good!

Dave Gilmour of Pink Floyd •110

A perfect record from start to finish – you couldn't improve on it.

George Harrison on Tina Turner's *River Deep, Mountain High,* masterfully produced by Phil Spector •111

Stylistically, I've always said that we can't be a heavy riff group because Led Zeppelin are the best in the world. We can't be a blues influenced R&B rock 'n' roll group because The Stones are the best in the world. We can't be a slightly sort of airy-fairy mystical synthesizing abstract freak-out group because Pink Floyd are the best in the world. And so what's left? And that's what we've always done. We've filled the gap. We've done what's left.

Ian Anderson explains Jethro Tull's niche •112

His tone is vocal; his ideas are superb; he plays almost exclusively blues – all the lines he plays in Cream are blues lines. He's a blues guitarist and he's taken blues guitar to its ultimate thing.

Mike Bloomfield on Eric Clapton •113

I always loved Roy. I looked up to the way he was, admired the way he handled himself. That aloofness he had influenced me profoundly.

Neil Young on Roy Orbison, 1990 •114

I wanted to make a record that would sound like Phil Spector. I wanted to write words like Dylan. I wanted my guitar to sound like Duane Eddy.

Bruce Springsteen 1987 •115

I should be sending Pete Townshend cards for Father's Day.

Eddie Vedder of Pearl Jam, 1995 •116

Since *New Boots and Panties* became the working man's *Tubular Bells*, Ian Dury has been adopted as some sort of mascot, as treasured and beloved an emblem as a battered teddy bear with a ripped ear and scorch marks on its fur.

Charles Shaar Murray 1979 •117

The Sex Pistols got it right, man; they made a good record, then blew up. I love that.

Chris Balew of The Presidents of the United States of America, 2000 •118

There's a real melancholy in [Abba's] songs...
all the flourishes, like big double octaves on
the piano, we stole them like crazy.

Elvis Costello 1991 •119

When I was about 14, I saw The Clash. I was pushed up
close and people were stage-diving, and there was this
sort of glorious, happy, violent chaos at work. It was like
an indoctrination to the pain of the pit. I guess I was a
little bit afraid, but I was also like, 'Well, actually, bring
it; I like my bruises.' It was a sweet kind of pain.

Stephan Jenkins of Third Eye Blind, 2001 •120

When I was a teenager, I loved The Buzzcocks,
Generation X, Elvis Costello, If you look at what those
artists sold, they weren't selling big in a world full of hack
artists that were selling millions and millions of records.

Matthew Sweet 2001 •121

My access to music when I was growing up was through pirate radio,
you know, transistor radio under the pillow, listening to one more
and then 'just one more' until your favourite track comes on.

Robert Palmer •122

When The Smiths came on Top Of The Pops for the first time, that was it for me. From that day on I wanted to be Johnny Marr.

Noel Gallagher of Oasis, 2000 •123

I get that tingle when I listen to Joy Division or The Smiths. There was something really weird going on with those bands, they created their own rules and life and aura.

Jimi Goodwin of The Doves, 2000 •124

When I saw The Stone Roses, I thought I could do that. And I did, didn't I?

Yes, Noel *you did.* 1994 •125

The first band I ever felt a part of were The Jam. I was a teenager and they were the best group in England. Paul Weller was the coolest pop singer. Totally. The Jam always had a single out every three months, which is what Oasis are trying to emulate.

Noel Gallagher of Oasis, 1994 •126

Even if I were talentless, after seeing Echo and The Bunnymen eight million times and Nirvana ten million times, how could I not write an okay new wave record?

Courtney Love of Hole, 1994 •127

Rob, top five musical crimes perpetuated by Stevie Wonder in the 80s and 90s. Go. Sub-question: is it in fact unfair to criticize a formerly great artist for his latter day sins, is it better to burn out or fade away?

Jack Black's Barry interrogates his boss (John Cusack) in *High Fidelity* (2000) •128

I have this huge catalogue of melodies in my head, and I've heard it all, the Merseybeat thing, late 60s psychedelic, glam rock, prog rock. I was there for it all. So that's all part of me. 'Guided by Voices' name refers to all those influences. That's what the voices are.

Bob Pollard of Guided By Voices, 2001 •129

I met Coldplay, and they were nice guys, But then I heard *Yellow* and thought, 'Oh, that's a big song. That's a huge song'

Fran Healy of Travis, 2001 •130

Homer Simpson: You know, my kids think you're the greatest. And thanks to your gloomy music, they've finally stopped dreaming of a future I can't possibly provide.

Billy Corgan: Well, we try to make a difference.

The Smashing Pumpkins frontman does a good deed •131

5

Why she had to go I don't know,
She wouldn't say
I said something wrong
Now I long for yesterday.

The Beatles *Yesterday*
(Lennon & McCartney),
(1965), from the album *Help!* •132

We don't think The Beatles will do anything in this market.

Head of Capitol records, Jay Livingstone in 1964 •133

There in the centre tunnel on a raised platform was a sight that galvanised him. It was in the most specific way a personification of his secret sexual desires. On stage were four young men dressed in leather trousers and jackets. They played good time rock and roll and joked with each other with macho camaraderie.

Peter Brown describes Brian Epstein's first visit to the Cavern Club in 1961 •134

I'm all for perfection as long as it doesn't take more than eight weeks because then it's a bore.

John Lennon 1974 •135

I wanted to manage those four boys. It wouldn't take me more than two half days a week.

Brian Epstein in 1961, after seeing The Beatles •136

To be frank, Mr Epstein, we don't like your boys' sound – groups of guitarists are on the way out.

Head of Decca records, Dick Rowe in 1962 •137

By the end of 1963, Brian Epstein was able to look back at a year in which his artists had dominated the hit parade with an incredible nine number ones, spanning 32 weeks at the top. No manager in British pop history has ever achieved comparable chart supremacy.

Johnny Rogan 1988 •138

We were all on this ship in the sixties, our generation, a ship going to discover the New World.
And The Beatles were in the crow's nest of that ship.

John Lennon 1974, quoted in *Imagine*, 1988 •139

They are, in my mind, responsible for most of the degeneration that has happened, not only musically but also in the sense of youth orientation and politically, too. They are the people who made it first publicly acceptable to spit in the eye of authority.

The Nazi manifesto? No, Frank Sinatra on The Beatles •140

Rock and roll isn't a form of entertainment. It's a culture, a civilisation. It has taken over the past half-century. There's never been anything like it. And here is a man who was one of the greatest masters of it, who embodies its essence. Aren't we going to learn something about this whole civilisation if we look at its leaders?

Albert Goldman •141

The very first tune I ever learn to play was *That'll Be the Day*. My mother taught me to play it on the banjo, sitting there with endless patience until I managed to work out all the chords.

John Lennon •142

One gets the impression they think simultaneously of harmony and melody, so firmly are the major tonic sevenths and ninths built into their tunes.

Walter Mann on Lennon & McCartney's songs in *The Times*, 1963 •143

I discovered the frabjous falsetto shriek-cum-croon, the ineluctable beat, the flawless intonation, the utterly fresh lyrics, the Schubert-like flow of musical invention, and the fuck-you coolness of these Four Horsemen of Our Apocalypse.

Leonard Bernstein 1979 •144

It is possible to see in The Beatles' music a synthesis in which one of the strongest elements has been a powerful and probably instinctive Englishry... which goes back... to pastoral pentatonic tunes and other revitalised archaisms. The Times leader column, 1967 •145

Rock 'n' roll is the music that inspired me to play music. There is nothing conceptually better than rock 'n' roll. No group, be it the Beatles, Dylan or the Stones have ever improved on *Whole Lotta Shakin'* for my money. Or maybe, like our parents, that's my period and I'll dig it and never leave it. John Lennon •146

The 12 songs on *Sgt. Pepper* set a new standard of achievement in popular music. It took only four months to record, at a cost of £100,000. It was so different and stunning to hear at first that when The Beach Boys' Brian Wilson first listened to it, he gave up work on his own forthcoming album, thinking that the quintessential album had already been made. Peter Brown •147

Oh, I get it.
You don't want to be cute any more.
Bob Dylan's reaction to *Sgt. Pepper's* •148

Forgive the Beatles; they just didn't know any better. How could they? What happened to them had not happened to anybody else before except Elvis, and look what happened to him.

Charles Shaar Murray •149

Reporter: Would you like to walk down the street without being recognised?
Lennon: We used to do that with no money in our pockets. There's no point to it.

John Lennon 1964 •150

Big bastards, that's what The Beatles were. You have to be a bastard to make it. And The Beatles were the biggest bastards on earth.

John Lennon 1980 •151

We're kidding you, we're kidding ourselves, we're kidding everybody. We don't take anything seriously except the money. John Lennon •152

There are a staggering number of similarities between Lennon and Elvis. The two greatest men in the history of rock 'n' roll, which is how I conceive of Elvis and Lennon, were both so much alike it came in for psychic essence. They are both momma's boys. They were very bluesy, melancholic, withdrawn people looking for powerful, dominating keepers to direct them and also protect them. Both drifting off into the world of drugs. Both taken up with fantasies of being Jesus, of coming back as the messiah, and all that. Very unfulfilled by their fame.

Albert Goldman 1988 •153

Christianity will go. It will vanish and shrink. I needn't argue about that. I'm right and I'll be proved right. We're more popular than Jesus now.

John Lennon 1966 •154

Politics was one of John's ways of struggling with being rich. In a sense, to John, being rich was selling out. He was by instinct part socialist, part right-wing Archie Bunker; to be an indolent, wealthy rock star would have made him feel as guilty as sin.

Peter Brown •155

My defences were so great. The cocky rock and roll hero who knows all the answers was actually a terrified guy who didn't know how to cry. Simple.

John Lennon *Playboy* 1980 •156

Lots of people who complained about us receiving the MBE received theirs for heroism in the war – for killing people. We received ours for entertaining other people. I'd say we deserve ours more.

John Lennon 1969 •157

On this trip John managed to surpass his previous craziness. One night he walked on stage naked with a toilet seat around his neck to the cheers of the audience.

Peter Brown on The Beatles' performances in Hamburg in 1961 •158

John Lennon had a profound intolerance of children, being too much of a child himself to tolerate any rivals

Albert Goldman •159

I didn't blame John or Yoko. I understood their love. I knew there was no way I could ever fight the unity of mind and body that they had with each other.

Cynthia Lennon •160

What would you think if I sang out of tune,
Would you stand up and walk out on me?

The Beatles *With A Little Help From My Friends*
(Lennon & McCartney) from the album *Sgt. Pepper's...* •161

I like that first John Lennon album a hell of a
lot. I think all the songs are really beautifully
written and very straight from the shoulder.
There's an honesty in the lyrics there.

David Bowie •162

I'm a smoke-screen expert. I lie all
the time. It is the price of fame.

Paul McCartney *The Observer* 1998 •163

McCartney is one of those people who everyone's got too much
attitude about. If you see how many lives pop music has destroyed
from a fleeting moment's fame, its kinda remarkable that he's still
so fluent. People forget what a good musician the guy is, what a
great rock 'n' roll singer.

Elvis Costello 1989 •164

We'll never get to that stage of releasing rubbish because we know people will buy it.

Paul McCartney 1965. *Frog Chorus* anyone? •165

I've never really done anything to create what has happened. It creates itself. I'm here because it happened. But I didn't do anything to make it happen other than saying 'Yes'

Ringo Starr •166

Does Ringo exist apart from his records? Who cares? It's doubtful the cutesy-pie tracks Richard Perry has turned into Ringo Records will ever move a listener to do anything more than reach for the radio dial and that's what's so unnerving about these records. These cuts – this *No No Song*, that thoughtless remake of *Only You*, *Oh My My*, *You're Sixteen* – they're maddening only for their lack of personality, depth, emotional commitment. They're so insubstantial they're hardly fit objects to provoke boredom, much less concern and despair.

Gene Sculatti March 1976 •167

I'm just a dog and I'm led around by me collar by Krishna.

George Harrison •168

After the spiritual life with George, within a few weeks of going to live with Eric I seemed to be surrounded by mayhem. I drank like a fish too.

Patti Harrison on life in the Clapton household •169

To be fair, the movie does show a certain charm in its relentlessly stupid grasp of the obvious. When Frampton sings *The Long and Winding Road*, for example, he is walking down a long and winding road. You keep laughing and thinking it can't get any worse. But it does.

Charles M. Young on Beatles movie *Sgt. Pepper's Lonely Hearts Club Band*, in *Rolling Stone* magazine, 1978 •170

His place in history was already reserved as the most luckless of all might-have-beens. In the next 24 months, The Beatles would gross £17 million. Pete Best became a banker, earning £8 a week, and married a girl named Kathy who worked at the biscuit counter at Woolworth's.

Peter Brown •171

Was I the fifth Beatle? Not really. George Best •172

I've met them. Delightful lads. Absolutely no talent.

6

THE ROCKER

I said 'Hey baby, meet me I'm a tough guy
Got my cycle outside, you wanna try?'
She just looked at me and rolled them big eyes
And said 'Ooh I'd do anything for you 'cause you're a rocker.'

Thin Lizzy *The Rocker* (1973) from the album
Vagabonds Of The Western World •174

69

You put a greased, naked woman on all fours, with a dog collar around her neck, and a leash, and the man's arm extended out up to here, holding on to the leash and pushing a black glove in her face to sniff it. You don't find that offensive?

Fran Deschler as Bobbi, debating Spinal Tap's new album cover (*This Is Spinal Tap*) (1984) •175

We were the first band ever to have big 4 x 12 cabinets. I was the first bass player to have two stacks, the first bass player to have two amps. We were the first really loud group.

John Entwistle of The Who 1974 •176

If you take everything in the universe and break it down to a common denominator, all you've got is energy. That's the essence of the urban sound.

Wayne Kramer of MC5 •177

Jimmy Page represented all that was ethereal, exquisite, divine, and pornographic in rock music...

Pamela Des Barres on the Led Zeppelin guitarist, 1989 •178

I wanted to be in a band that gave bang for the buck. I wanted to be in the band who didn't look like a bunch of guys who, you know, should be in a library studying for their finals.

Gene Simmons of Kiss •179

Imagine living in *Das Boot* for five years.

Henry Rollins on his time in Black Flag, 1994 •180

I remember arguing with him once, after a few whiskeys… next thing I know, I got my teeth knocked out. That's how he led the band.

Lynyrd Skynyrd's Billy Powell on Steve Van Zandt's leadership technique •181

It's just rock and roll. A lot of times we get criticised for it. A lot of music papers come out with: 'When are they going to stop playing these three chords?' If you believe you shouldn't play just three chords it's pretty silly on their part. To us, the simpler a song is, the better, 'cause it's more in line with what the person on the street is. Angus Young of AC/DC in the *Atlanta Gazette*, 1980 •182

AC/DC's *Highway to Hell* is the greatest meshing of vocal, guitar and content I've ever heard. That's what I aspire to.

Bonnie Raitt 2000 •183

If it was happening, I'd call it Heavenly Beast. If it wasn't happening, I usually call it Asshole.

Angus Young in *Rolling Stone,* on being asked if his guitar had a name •184

Cooper is a master charlatan; indeed, he has elevated charlatanry to a higher artistic plane than anybody else in rock and roll had ever dreamed of.

Charles Shaar Murray on Alice Cooper •185

Fuck Elvis and Keith Richards! Lemmy's the king of rock 'n' roll. He's a living, breathing, drinking and snorting fucking legend. No one else comes close.

Foo Fighters' **Dave Grohl** on Lemmy, 2006 •186

I took *Spinal Tap* real personal. I was really high at the time and Aerosmith was sinking – we were like a boat going down. And that movie was way too close, way too real.

Steven Tyler of Aerosmith, 1990 •187

It's almost like we'd get worried if we got a good review. My daughter's homework reports are better than our reviews.

Steve Harris of Iron Maiden •188

Whoever you name, Dave Lee Roth was undoubtedly the most over-the-top, larger-than-life rock star you could ever hope to meet. **Mick Wall** on Van Halen's main man •189

Metallica is just four lucky friends that got together and started playing… this could be you!

James Hetfield of Metallica •190

**But we'll never stop
We'll never quit
'Cos we're Metallica'**

Metallica *Whiplash* (1983) from the album *Ride The Lightning* •191

Bon Jovi are a kind of simpleton's version of heavy rock. Their messages, about love, friendship or life on the road, are big and generalised. Corny, even.

Adam Sweeting •192

We're like a fuckin' grenade and it's like everybody's struggling to hold the pin in!

Slash of Guns N' Roses, 1988 •193

I don't care if you think I'm being big-headed. This is the only rock'n'roll band to come out of LA that's real.

Slash •194

It's just such cool chemistry between us. We've been together for so long and care about each other so much, it's really like brothers.

Adam Yauch of Beastie Boys, 1998 •195

The first thing I remember of Pearl Jam was hearing 'Alive' on the radio while I was living in Seattle. I pictured Mountain or some serious '70s throwback. The music just seemed like classic rock to me, so I pictured the singer being some husky, fuckin' bearded, leather-jacketed Tad type. Big and fat and tortured and scary.

Dave Grohl of Nirvana and The Foo Fighters, 2001 •196

This hi-wattage trio doesn't seem to belong to Geffen, but this is combative, heavy-hitting rock that thinks on its feet. Slightly Pixies-like, but less whimsical. Big in '92. Adam Sweeting on the release of *Nevermind* in 1991. Clever boy. •197

Nirvana slayed the hair bands. They shot the top off the poodles. All of a sudden, all those bands like Poison, Bon Jovi and Warrant became like Rommel in the desert: overextended, bloated, no more Vaseline. And now they're just rusty tanks in the desert with no gas. Nirvana is going to be remembered for changing the face of rock. Henry Rollins 1994 •198

Don't talk to me about Nirvana. He was a sad man who couldn't handle the fame. We're stronger than that. And you can fuck your fucking Pearl Jam.

Liam Gallagher sensitive soul, 1994 •199

It wasn't always comfortable competing against Nirvana, and it was certainly not healthy living under that shadow at times. But at least there was honour in it. We all respected that it was a great band – Pearl Jam too. But competing against Bush? It's nothing to get your dick hard about, you know what I mean? There's no mojo in that!

Billy Gallagher of The Smashing Pumpkins, 1996 •200

I know nothing about rock and roll. Do you know, until recently I thought that Led Zeppelin sang *Smoke On The Water?* Justine Frischmann
of Elastica, 1994 •201

I guess it's like folk music, only really loud.

Mark Louris of The Jayhawks describing his band's sound, 1995 •202

It's basically angry bubblegum.

Dave Wyndori of Monster Magnet, 2001 •203

I started rapping because I couldn't fucking sing.

Coby Dick of Papa Roach, 2000 •204

You're seeing black people at metal shows and white people at hip-hop shows. Everything's starting to melt together. Fred Durst of Limp Bizkit •205

You wonder why we sound the way we do? We were born in scum, we live in filth and we die in dirt. Max Cavalera of Sepultura •206

I turn on the TV and there's this band, tattoos, shirts off... I laugh at first, but then I get kind of sad. People really think this is the alternative. It's a bunch of millionaires pretending to be bad boys, pretending to be pivotal components of youth.

John Reis of Rocket From The Crypt, 2001 •207

I'm just a regular guy, you know? There's no leotard and cape under my clothes. I shit, I piss, I drink too much and throw up, just like everybody else.

Chester Bennington of Linkin Park, 2001 •208

This tragic bombardment of tuneless metal cliché fails to move in any direction other than towards the bin.

Steve Beebee on Debase's album *Domination,* in *Kerrang,* October 2001 •209

Macho rap-rock from the UK. Horrible, horrible. This is the sound of five men in competition to prove who has the most testosterone.

Emma Johnston on nu-metal bank Lillydamnwhite (album *Eviscerate*) in *Kerrang,* July 2001 •210

The still-born brainchild of Korn bassist Reginald Fieldy Arvizu, *Rock 'n' Roll Gangster* is an utterly unlikeable gangsta-rap pastiche. When not tiresomely trumpeting his titanic weed intake, Fieldy stumbles through sterilised sex rhymes and banal B-boy bragging so devoid of charm or wit that they make the similarly salacious Kid Rock sound like Stephen Fry in comparison.

Dan Silver on the album *Rock 'n' Roll Gangster* by Fieldy's Dreams, in *Q* magazine, January 2002 •211

Three tracks in this truly lamentable opus and you'll have lost the will to live; four tracks and you'll be weeping openly into your coffee cup.

James Cooper on heavy metal band Solstice's album *Lamentations* in *Kerrang,* August 2001 •212

All rock musicians are deaf...
Or insensitive to mellow sounds.

Marc Bolan •213

Of all the things I've lost, it's my mind I miss the most.

Ozzy Osbourne •214

SYMPATHY FOR THE DEVIL

7

**Please allow me to introduce myself,
I'm a man of wealth and taste,
I've been around for a long, long year,
Stole many a man's soul and faith.**

Rolling Stones *Sympathy For The Devil* (1968)
from the album *Beggars Banquet* •215

...the combo they writhe and twist to is called The Rolling Stones. Maybe you've never heard of them – if you live far from London, the odds are you haven't. But, by gad, you will! Norman Jopling of the *Record Mirror* reviews the Stones' 1962 gig at the Crawdaddy •216

For most people, the fantasy is driving around in a big car, having all the chicks you want and being able to pay for it. It always has been, still is, and always will be. And anyone who says it isn't is talking bullshit.

Mick Jagger •217

Mick Jagger is the greatest performer since Nijinsky.

Patti Smith •218

He moves like a parody between a majorette girl and Fred Astaire.

Truman Capote on Mick Jagger •219

I think rock 'n' roll is all frivolity – it should be about pink satin suits and white socks.

Mick Jagger •220

Mick Jagger is the perfect pop star.
There's nobody more perfect than Jagger.
He is rude, he's ugly-attractive, he's brilliant.
The Rolling Stones are the perfect pop
group – they don't give a shit. Elton John •221

I wanted to be an actress, and a scholar too. My first move was to get a Rolling Stone as a boyfriend. I slept with three, then decided that the singer was the best.

Marianne Faithfull •222

Rock and roll is the rhythm of our generation. It is the epitome of the kind of rhythm our generation grew up with, it is very natural to them. As long as this generation carries on, rock 'n' roll will live with it. But now there's a new generation and it's searching for its own rhythm. Each generation has its own rhythm. Our parents had swing, we had rock and the kids of today are taking our stuff and interpreting it for their time and for their feeling of life.

Keith Richards 1991 •223

I never liked *Revolver* very much. I don't like the Beatles. I'm not saying that I never liked anything they did and I'm not saying that they didn't influence me, because it's impossible not to be influenced by them. Mick Jagger 1974 •224

The Rolling Stones. It took the people from England to hip my people – my white people – to what they had in their own backyard. That sounds funny, but it's the truth. Muddy Waters •225

In 1963, Andrew Loog Oldham became The Rolling Stones' manager. Oldham, without doubt, was the most flash personality that British pop has ever had, the most anarchic and obsessive and imaginative hustler of all. Whenever he was good, he was quite magnificent. Nik Cohn •226

Actually, if you're a musician I think it's very good not to be with anybody and just live on your own. Domesticity is death. Mick Jagger 1974 •227

Narcissism and arrogance, concisely set out in *Get off My Cloud*, are the keynote of most of The Stones' lyrics.

Alan Beckett in *New Left Review,* 1967 •228

Mick's an old friend of mine. Our battles aren't exactly what people think they are. There are many different levels – it's not just 'who runs The Rolling Stones?' Keith Richards 1988 •229

I don't want audiences to be in awe. I just want them to have a good time. With Woody, the band is more good-timey. Mick Jagger on bandmate Ronnie Wood, 1976 •230

I'm sick of playing places like Madison Square Garden. I want to play some small towns. I'm sick of playing places where everyone in the audience looks as good, or better, than I do. Keith Richards 1973 •231

I've been asked if this is the last tour since I was 19 years old.

Mick Jagger •232

Let it be acknowledged: there are very few performers in the world who could dominate a vast audience of 20,000 as he did. Narcissist, freak, dandy, dancer, rocker, God, devil, stripper, sensualist, tease – the women in the audience are not there for the popcorn – Mr Jagger at 38 is still a kind of wild animal. His athleticism, the result of jogging several miles a day, is phenomenal. He has become the Nureyev of rock 'n' roll.

John Heilpern on The Rolling Stones at Madison Square Garden in 1981 •233

I'd rather be dead than singing *Satisfaction* when I'm 45.

Mick Jagger 45, no way, but 61 is cool •234

At the Grammy Awards, Keith Richards became the first performer ever to accept a posthumous award in Britain.

Jay Leno *The Tonight Show*, NBC •235

I heard Muddy Waters play six months before he died and he was as powerful and strong as ever. So I say, good, let's find out. It's an uncharted area now for a rock 'n' roll band to go on this far. I'm looking forward to it – there's a sort of Columbus feel about it.

Keith Richards 1991 •236

I hope to be half as cool as The Stones for half as long.

Jon Bon Jovi 1989 •237

It's all right letting your self go, as long as you can get your self back.

Mick Jagger •238

TEENAGE KICKS

8

I need excitement oh I need it bad,
And it's the best I've ever had.
I wanna hold her wanna hold her tight,
Get teenage kicks right through the night.

Undertones *Teenage Kicks* (1978) •239

I asked a ouija board once if I'd ever be in a rock band. It said no, and I was crushed.

Fred Schneider of The B-52's •240

One of the things which has impressed me most in life was the Mod movement in England, which was an incredible youthful thing. It was a movement of young people, much bigger than the hippy thing, the underground and all these things. It was an army, a powerful, aggressive army of teenagers with transport.

Pete Townshend •241

That's all I wanted to do as a kid. Play a guitar properly and jump around.

Syd Barrett 1971 •242

To the outside adult eye, Punk Rock is the weirdest, ugliest, nastiest, scariest, most thoroughly repulsive and flat-out incomprehensible variant on the Teenage Wasteland formula that they've ever seen.

Charles Shaar Murray 1977 •243

At its best New Wave/punk represents a fundamental and age-old Utopian dream: that if you give people the license to be as outrageous as they want in absolutely any fashion they can dream up, they'll be creative about it, and do something good besides.

Lester Bangs in *NME,* 1977 •244

Some people have wives and girlfriends. I had the New York Dolls.

Morrissey quoted in *Mojo* 2006 •245

The Ramones are pocket punks, a perfect razor edged bubblegum band. They should never make an album. They should make a single every week, 'cos they've already got enough songs to last them for the first six months.

Charles Shaar Murray in the *NME* 1975 •247

Nobody's gonna like you guys, but I'll have you back.

Hilly Kristal owner of CBGB, to The Ramones after their first audition 1974 •246

If it wasn't for The Ramones, or Joey in particular, there wouldn't be a Green Day, an Offspring, a Rancid, a Blink 182 – there wouldn't be any punk band, period. There are bands that are influenced by The Ramones that don't even know it yet.

Billie Joe Armstrong of Green Day, 2001 •248

Up on the roof, out on the street
Down in the playground, the hot concrete,
Bus ride is too slow,
They blast out the disco on the radio

The Ramones *Rockaway Beach* (1977) from the album *Rocket To Russia* •249

They were musically, culturally, in every way, the best thing in the world.

Tony Wilson on The Sex Pistols •250

No one in this band is a musician.
We all hate the term. We're something
close to factory – workers. Machinists.
Skilled operators.

John Lydon (as Johnny Rotten), quoted in *Rock'n'Roll Babylon,* 1982 •251

Punks in their silly leather jackets are a cliché. I never liked the term and have never discussed it. I just got on with it and got out of it when it became a competition. **John Lydon** *The Observer*, 1986 •252

I don't have to be pretentious or fake to impress anyone around me because they all know exactly what I am. A big fake cunt.

John Lydon of Public Image Ltd. 1998 •253

It wasn't like, 'These guys are great!' the thought was, 'Fuckin' A! if these wankers can make music, we can make music.' Thing was, The Sex Pistols were funny. Punks knew they looked ridiculous.

Bernard Sumner of New Order, 1993 •254

Ziggy Stardust had a mutant bastard offspring and his name was Johnny Rotten. **David Bowie** 1980 •255

Richard Branson doesn't even invite me round his house no more. That's because I usually beg for money and I hate cricket. **John Lydon** •256

When I was about 14, I saw The Clash. I was pushed up close and people were stage-diving, and there was this sort of glorious, happy, violent chaos at work. It was like an indoctrination to the pain of the pit. I guess I was a little bit afraid, but I was also like, 'Well, actually, bring it; I like my bruises.' It was a sweet kind of pain.

Stephan Jenkins of Third Eye Blind, 2001 •257

We weren't misogynistic. We were misanthropic.

Jean – Jacques Burnel of The Stranglers •258

My earliest memory is pretending to be dead. My mum used to step over me while I was laying on the kitchen floor. Siouxsie Sioux of Siouxsie and The Banshees, 1993 •259

Mostly, punk was funny. We couldn't believe we were getting away with it.

Peter Shelley. of The Buzzcocks, 2001 •260

I hated most of the punk bands. There was only
The Pistols and The Clash that I really liked. I thought
the rest were fucking rubbish. It's all right getting all
dewy-eyed and nostalgic, but it was fucking awful.

Paul Weller ex- The Jam, 1994 •261

We were the dustmen of punk.

Jimmy Pursey of Sham 69 •262

I try to talk in tune. That's what I do, talk in tune.

John Cooper Clarke •263

The thing about The Cure is that we exist in isolation.
We're not in competition with anyone. One day
I suppose we'll stop. But we'll never be replaced.

Robert Smith 1989 •264

I wasn't born to follow
I live just for today, don't care about tomorrow
What I've got in my head you can't buy steal or borrow
I believe in live and let live
I believe you get what you give.

Primal Scream *Higher Than The Sun*, (Gillespie/Innes/Young) (1991),
from the album *Screamadelica* •265

Rent a flat above a shop,
Cut your hair and get a job,
Smoke some fags and play some pool,
Pretend you never went to school,
But still you'll never get it right.

Pulp *Common People* (1995), from the album *A Different Class* •266

I wish I could have taken a class on becoming a Rock Star. It might have prepared me for this.

Kurt Cobain •267

My generation's apathy. I'm disgusted with it. I'm disgusted with my own apathy too, for being spineless and not always standing up against racism, sexism and all those other – isms the counterculture has been whining about for years.

Kurt Cobain •268

Punk is musical freedom. It's saying, doing and playing what you want. In Webster's terms, 'nirvana' means freedom from pain, suffering and the external world, and that's pretty close to my definition of Punk Rock.

Kurt Cobain •269

What people have got to understand is that we are lads. We have burgled houses and nicked car stereos, and we like girls and we swear and we go to the football and we take the piss.

Noel Gallagher prompting a police investigation into banal utterances in 1996 •270

There has to be danger, we have to instil a sense of fear in the audience and in ourselves.

Trent Reznor of Nine Inch Nails •271

I don't think what I do is original at all. It's more out of faithfulness to my adolescent dreams that I'm still doing this.

Rivers Cuomo of Weezer, 2000 •272

I grew up as a rebellious kid who was always locked up in his room. When I got out, I wasn't bad – I just didn't know what was right or wrong.

Fred Durst of Limp Bizkit, 1999 •273

**We're not your average American band.
We're not shit heads.** Mike Dirnt of Green Day •274

I think it's your own choice if you turn from an angry young man
to a bitter, old bastard, or if you stay hungry in a good way.
Billie Joe Armstrong of Green Day, 2000 •275

**We're not a political band and we don't want
to tell people what to do or what to think.**
Billie Joe Armstrong 1997 •276

**If I could see one band that I never got to see, it would
be Stiff Little Fingers. They were one of the first punk
rock bands I ever heard, and they're partially responsible
for me even playing guitar.** Tom DeLonge of Blink 182, 2001 •277

I guess it's all just music the way I look at it. It's hard to
call it rock & roll anymore... I think rock & roll is dead.
Billie Joe Armstrong 1995 •278

**We made it easy for them to come and nick things
from us. They're sticky tape on a duck's arse.**
John Lydon questions Green Day's originality •279

My mom used to tell me when I was a kid, 'If you curse at night-time, the devil's going to come to you when you're sleeping.' I used to get excited because I really wanted it to happen… I wanted it more than anything.

Marilyn Manson 1998 •280

Marilyn Manson is like a train wreck or a long form of suicide and people live vicariously through it. Sometimes I do things a lot of people wish they could do. If they don't wish they could do it, they enjoy being amused by it or being disgusted by it.

Marilyn Manson 1998 •281

He's ruthless, Machiavellian and great fun to be around. Humour isn't something that's normally associated with Marilyn Manson, but he's got an extremely dry wit.

Brian Molko of Placebo, 2000 •282

Eminem, he's good. Intense – intense and committed. He's got a lot to say and he says it. Vehemently. `Bruce Springsteen` 2003 •283

I'm just a regular motherfucker. I'm Marshal Mathers before I'm Slim Shady, before I'm Eminem, before I'm anybody. `Eminem` 2000 •284

Slim Shady is just another part of me, the dark, evil, creatively sick part.

`Eminem` •285

God sent me to piss off the world.

`Eminem` 2000 •286

Musicians who didn't pay attention to punk have a gap in their knowledge that makes it difficult to communicate in this day and age.

Flea of The Red Hot Chili Peppers, 1992 •287

Being punk rock is not having to prove you are. It's obvious to anyone who is authentic in that mindset. You don't have to call yourself a punk rocker.

Thurston Moore of Sonic Youth 1994 •288

Country music is completely punk-rock. It's the original punk-rock.

Neko Case •289

Don't you think it's about time I grew up? I'm 43-years old, man.

Bob Pollard of Guided By Voices, 2001 •290

BURNING SKY

9

We've all grown up and we've got our own lives
And the values that we had once upon a time,
Seem useless now 'cos the rent must be paid,
And some bonds severed and others made.

The Jam *Burning Sky,* (Weller) (1979)
from the album *Setting Sons* •291

It's really sad that rock, especially alternative rock, has become corporate business.

Billy Corgan of The Smashing Pumpkins 1995 •292

I have this feeling record companies used to have more music lovers working for them. Rather than all bankers the way it is now – mostly bankers.

Evan Dando of The Lemonheads 1996 •293

What pisses me off is when I've got seven or eight record company fat pig men sitting there telling me what to wear.

Sinead O'Connor 1997 •294

I like the music business because as horrible an empire as it is and as tacky as it is, it's always in transition. They try to control things as much as they can but they can't – as much as they race around after it. And I like watching that because it's a real microcosm of society. You can't really control it. The safest thing is just to be aware of what is going on.

Thurston Moore of Sonic Youth, circa 1995 •295

In England everybody is trying to make money but they're ashamed to admit it. Here it's easy to talk business.

Jon Moss of Culture Club finds New York more to his taste •296

Music is spiritual.
The music business is not.

Van Morrison *The Times*, 1990 •297

Most bands don't make money. They just squander it on producers and cocaine and lots of other bullshit, and it's disgusting. There's so much idiotic excess. It goes beyond enjoyment.

Sting •298

Rock never managed to die before it got old. Instead, it put on a bit of weight and became part of the showbusiness mainstream.

Adam Sweeting 1986 •299

There are two kinds of artists left; those who endorse Pepsi and those who simply won't.

Annie Lennox 1990 •300

I hate the industry even more now, no bands get nurtured anymore. Labels only spend money promoting acts they know will be Top Ten. I find it offensive spending $2 million on a video.

Siouxsie Sioux •301

What the major companies have done in the last few years is find out that they couldn't find any more Whitesnakes. They took a look at their marketing budget and put it behind hip-hop and figured out how to make it pop.

Chuck D •302

The rock music business is a cruel and shallow trench, a long plastic hallway where thieves and pimps run free, and good men die like dogs. There is also a negative side.

Hunter S Thompson •303

He would bring me into his office and play me 16 different test pressings that only dogs could hear the differences on.

Bob Krasnow on Phil Spector's search for perfection on *River Deep, Mountain High* •304

I don't consider Motown black – I consider them half and half. Black people making white music.

Phil Spector •305

Phil had been trying to construct this giant wall of sound ever since he got started in the record business, and when he heard me, he knew that my voice was the final brick.

Ronnie Spector •306

The studio is an instrument, manipulate it, don't go in thinking it's got to sound like my band. When I got done with *Pretty Gate Machine*, I realized, 'Holy fuck, how am I going to play this live?'

Trent Reznor of Nine Inch Nails, 1996 •307

It's a radical time for musicians, a really revolutionary time, and I believe revolutions like Napster are a lot more fun than cash, which by the way we don't have at major labels anyway, so we might as well get with it and get in the game. Courtney Love •308

Treating your audience like thieves is absurd. Anyone who chooses to listen to our music becomes a collaborator.

Jeff Tweedy •309

This is the end of an era in pop music. It's the end of ideology. Everything is branded. It began with the compilation album – music to drive to, music to eat to, – thus denying each artist their own ideological spirit. Pop is now given away with a few Esso coupons at your local garage. Malcolm McLaren *The Observer,* 1998 •310

Whenever you can buy hamburgers to your favourite songs, you know it's over.

Peter Buck of R.E.M., circa 1996 •311

If you look at the radio playlists of virtually every commercial station modern rock, alternative or whatever, there's practically no independent music at all. They don't just say, 'Hey this is cool, we'll play this.' It's a political, calculated thing. It all comes down to label support, and most independent labels don't have the kind of backing it takes to break a record in that environment.

Warren Fitzgerald of The Vandals, 2000 •312

Promoting pop music ain't about nothing but whores and blow.

Steve Earle 2000 •313

The key to building a superstar is to keep their mouth shut. To reveal an artist to the people can be to destroy him.

Bob Ezrin producer •314

Every time there was an interview, it was Malcolm who was being interviewed, not us. And that wasn't what it was all about. Not for me anyway.

Glen Matlock in his autobiography, *I Was a Teenage Sex Pistol,* 1990 •315

If Adam [Ant] was the first of the artists as businessmen then McLaren was the businessman as artist. He didn't play the guitar, but he did play the media. More interested in an adventure than a career, he was in some respects an awful manager. He just didn't care. No good going to him if you were looking for a future in the pop game. He'd drop you as soon as he got bored. Dave Rimmer •316

Now you can manufacture just about what you want and after just a little time the artist is forgotten and gone.

Jimmy Cliff •317

See her picture in a thousand places 'cause she's this year's girl. You think you all own little pieces of this year's girl.

Elvis Costello *This Year's Girl,* (1978) from the album *This Year's Model* •318

It will be massive! It will jump out of the box and go mad. It will explode! Believe me – I know.

Terence Trent D'Arby predicts great things for his 1989 album *Neither Fish Nor Flesh.* It sucked and it sunk. •319

You can never tell if your fans will like an album or if they won't and I'm not gonna sit and try to market myself to anybody.

Billie Joe Armstrong of Green Day 2001 •320

MTV is pathetic. We have no place on it... I would almost rather say I don't want to be on the fuckin' thing.

Billie Joe Armstrong 1995 •321

By MTV trying to visualise the music they automatically stripped it of most of its natural mystery and depth. Before rock video, when people were confronted by the music, they had to rely on their own natural ability to utilise their imagination.

Neil Young 1990 •322

I think you're in trouble if your videos are better than your songs.

Boy George •323

Rock journalism is people who can't write interviewing people who can't talk for people who can't read.

Frank Zappa •325

I see a lot of people willingly and unwillingly having idiosyncrasies in their lives magnified into freak elements simply to land the cover of magazines.

Bob Mould of Sugar, ex-Husker Du, 1996 •326

There is nothing at all the matter with some journalists that a quick slap in the face couldn't sort out.

Elvis Costello 1995 •327

Most journalists shouldn't have a job. Most papers are a waste of time. A waste of trees. Futile. I'd rather read a tree. You'd even get bowel cancer if you use those papers as toilet roll.

Shane MacGowan 1989 •328

If you give one magazine an interview, then the other magazine wants an interview. If you give one to one, then the other one wants one. So pretty soon, you're in the interview business... You're just giving interviews...

Bob Dylan 1969 •329

The media over-estimates its own importance. I was on the cover of everything for three years, but I still only had half a bottle of milk in the fridge.

Mark E Smith of The Fall •330

Fame makes a man take things over,
Fame lets him loose, hard to swallow,
Fame puts you there where things are hollow.

David Bowie *Fame,* (co-written with John Lennon) (1975) from the album *Young Americans* •331

The Doors, in their success, did little more than pretend to provoke the imagination. They were wholly and obviously synthetic.

Sandy Pearlman •332

I think when you become successful it's very easy to step over and become product, and that has never happened and will never happen to me.

Morrissey circa 1994 •333

Celebrity fucks people up. Celebrity knocks the stuffing out of people, personally and creatively. There's not much that fucks you up faster than celebrity and isolation.

George Michael *Bare* magazine, 1988 •334

It's kind of hip to complain about success.

Scott Weiland of Stone Temple Pilots 1993 •335

If you're in jazz and more than ten people like you, you're labelled commercial.

Herbie Mann •336

Fame, on its best day, is kind of like a friendly wave from the stranger by the side of the road. And when it's not so good, it's like a long walk home, all alone, with nobody in when you get there.

Bruce Springsteen circa 1985 •337

I don't want to be recognized, I don't want to be hassled. I just want to play guitar in a rock and roll band.

Chrissie Hynde of The Pretenders 1995 •338

I'm famous now because of unhappiness. Your misery is everyone else's entertainment.

Adam Duritz of Counting Crows 1994 •339

It's all a bit overwhelming and I just need to chill out at home. I wasn't born yesterday, but I didn't realize how cutthroat it was.

Gavin Rossdale of Bush 1996 •340

The very weird religion of celebrity scares me. It's like people are creating fake heroes because they don't have any real ones. The politicians have failed us, religion has failed as, so who do people turn to? Celebrities. It is wrong. Michael Stipe 1992 •341

I get worried about the scale of success. Because basically I'm a very private person and I don't get a thrill from seeing my picture in the paper.

Mike Scott of The Waterboys •342

It's not like if The Jam had failed I could go and lay carpets. I'd be totally fucked. I'd probably still be sat in the pub on the estate, getting drunk.

Paul Weller March 2006 •343

I don't feel guilty for being rich and famous.

Sting 1996 •344

Just because you're successful, doesn't make you any wiser.

The Edge •345

As soon as you get any success you disappear up your own arse – and lose it forever.

Thom Yorke •346

I always wished for this, but it's almost turning into more of a nightmare than a dream.

Eminem on the price of fame •347

This fame thing. I don't get it I wrap my hand in plastic to try to look through it.

R.E.M. *E-Bow The Letter,* (1996) from the album *New Adventures in Hi-fi* •348

I used to be afraid of being in my 40s. Now I find out my 40s are pretty good. Of course, I'm rich and I'm married to Christie Brinkley, and that will tend to skew one's view of things.

Billy Joel •349

Financially, I want to be big in America, because that means I'll never have to work again. But it's not important to me to be a big star. It's more important to be big in England, because that's where I live, that's where I come from.

Noel Gallager of Oasis, 1996 •350

All artists go through a period of turmoil where they turn on success or success turns on them. Most of them can't ride that out. I guess I was fortunate in that I had been playing and singing for 13 years when success came. It touched me deeply but it didn't make me crazy. Roy Orbison 1988 •351

We've always known that we'd be huge stars, and it's all we wanted, so it won't surprise us when it happens. We don't want to be known as some fucking spaced out Mancunians who've got nothing better to do than take drugs and make music. **Ian Brown** of The Stone Roses, 1989 •352

His big stumbling block has been the problem that every major pop success faces and hardly anyone solves: when you've made your millions, when you've cut your monsters, when your peak has just been passed, what happens next? What about the 50 years before you die?

Nik Cohn on Phil Spector •353

There's no point in success if you don't let it go to your head. That's what it's for.

John Otway 1990 •354

It's a great story, isn't it? Loads of potential and, er, screwed up dramatically.

John Perry of The Only Ones •355

10

Just can't wait to get on the road again,
The life I love is makin' music with my friends.
Canned Heat *On The Road Again,* (1968) from
the album *Boogie With Canned Heat* •356

A lot of people don't like the road, but it's as natural to me as
breathing. I do it because I'm driven to do it, and I either hate
it or love it. I'm mortified to be on the stage, but then again,
it's the only place where I'm happy. Bob Dylan 1997 •357

ON THE ROAD AGAIN

I love my job. I love the position I'm in. I love
all the benefits that come with it; but I still
hate touring. Michael Stipe of R.E.M. 1994 •358

Onstage, I've been hit by a grapefruit, beer cans, eggs,
spit, money, cigarette butts, mandies, Quaaludes, joints,
bras, panties and a fist. Iggy Pop 1986 •359

I love to hear the crowd sing along. I get the biggest hard-on from that. Of course, it means I have an erection for a whole hour every night.

Chester Bennington of Linkin Park 2001 •360

When I'm on the stage, I'm not in control of myself at all. I don't even know who I am. I'm not this rational person who can sit here now and talk to you. If you walked on the stage with a microphone in the middle of the concert, I'd probably come close to killing you.

Pete Townshend 1982 •361

It was good fun except old Van is such a miserable old fucker. It's amazing 'cos he got us on that tour. We were right down there on the list, but it was him who got us on. But d'you know, not once on that tour did he ever just poke his head round the dressing-room door and say, 'All right fellas?'

Nick Lowe 1979 •362

We can't stop touring because we like it so much. I believe I'm going nuts at times – but so what?

Ozzy Osbourne in his Black Sabbath days •363

The funny thing about touring is that you rehearse all the wrong things: the music, the stage show. That stuff isn't the problem, it's the other 22 hours of the day. That's the weird part. Michael Hutchence in 1991 •364

It's nice that you can go to any country, and all these people have been waiting to see you for six months, they bought the ticket ages ago. It's quite moving really. But it's strange when you come back to your little life in London. Darryl Hunt of The Pogues in 1991 •365

One of the papers said what a sad existence I must have, that I don't have a social life. But I do have a social life. Our floor in the hotel is like a little street in suburbia. We all pop in to see each other and have a cup of tea. It's just like when I was living in a squat, only now I make a lot more money.

Boy George on tour in Japan •366

The ultimate sin of any performer is contempt for the audience. Lester Bangs in *Village Voice,* 1977 •367

If you ever plan to motor west
Travel my way, take the highway that's the best
And get your kicks on Route 66.

Route 66, written by Bobby Troup performed by many •368

Would you put your lighters away? You're not at Elton John.

Noel Gallagher at Earl's Court in 1995, as Oasis play the anthemic *Womderwall* •369

Americans want grungy fucking people, stabbing themselves in the head on stage. They get a bright bunch like us, with deodorant on, they don't get it.

Liam Gallagher in 1997 •370

It means going into training. Then on the wagon for three months. I knew when I got back on stage, I'd enjoy it. But performing's like sex. You might like it, but you don't want to do it non-stop.

Mick Jagger in 1981 •371

If it wasn't the feeling I get while performing, I think it would have been impossible for me to have continued as long as I have.

Chuck Berry in his autobiography •372

There's nothing like being on stage. You can't put it in words. When the lights hit you, there's a certain spirit you feel. I don't like coming off!

Michael Jackson •373

That's one of the best feelings on the market, when you walk up the steps to the stage. It feels like sparks flying through you. I get tears in my eyes and – I know this sounds really schmaltzy – but I just want to give.

Michael Hutchence •374

It's a pretty cool feeling going out there and seeing 70,000 smiling faces. Greatest feeling in the world.

Jon Bon Jovi •375

With it's dozen strong dance troupe, set piece dialogues, elaborate costumes and multiple sets, including a Metropolis-style futuristic nightmare, a cathedral, a harem and a Thirties nightclub, Madonna's *Blonde Ambition* is a Broadway musical in all essentials except for its lack of plot. Charles Shaar Murray in 1990 •376

I tried to make the show accommodate my own short attention span. Madonna on the same show •377

When we first started playing, I'd go into every show expecting nobody to come, and I'd go on stage expecting nobody to give me anything for free. And that's the way you have to play. If you don't play like that, pack your guitar up, throw it in a trash can and go home, fix televisions or some other line of work, ya know?

Bruce Springsteen in 1981 •378

There are perfectly sane men and women who will tell you that those first Rainbow Roxy Music concerts changed their lives; the presentation, the cleverness, the stylisation, the audience.

Peter York •379

Olympia is like many large concert venues: when fully packed it closely resembles the concentration camp scenes in Wertmuller's Seven Beauties. A greyish darkness piled with sullen, lumpy half dead whelps.

Lester Bangs at a Wings concert in 1976 •380

The Waterboys crowd is a riotous assembly of time warped punks, stubbly young men of poetic aspect in loose-fitting shirts and long hair, people clearly familiar with the clubs and pubs where traditional music is played, and others who can only be described as parents. All that was really lacking was a Guinness fountain.

Adam Sweeting in 1989 •381

Suede's confidence implied that the identity dilemma will be quickly resolved. Their swaggering sense of presence already makes them worth the price of admission. As we left, a girl cried, 'I touched him'. You can't buy that sort of credibility.

Caroline Sullivan in 1992 •382

Being on tour sends me crazy, I drink too much and out comes the John McEnroe in me.

The Pretenders' Chrissie Hynde •383

Pop concerts are just gatherings of people who want to have a good time and I don't think they really have a higher meaning.

Mick Jagger 1968 •384

I don't want to be a caricature of myself.

Singer Tom Jones asks women not to throw underwear at him during concerts •385

Things do sometimes get a little out of hand around me. I remember this show where I was grabbed and held down, while one chick was trying to pull my pants down. Some others were trying to french kiss me. And another one used her mouth on me. All the time I'd be kicking one, hitting another. I like to fight chicks. It turns me on.

Iggy Pop 1972 •386

I really do love performing. I mean it, it's totally natural to me, I'm a dandy, a show-off. I get very high on all the attention. I love it.

Freddie Mercury 1974 •387

If I leave the stage feeling, 'Well if I played just one more song, maybe somebody out there would be won over', if I feel I could have given more it's hard for me to sleep that night.

Bruce Springsteen 1981 •388

I couldn't talk to people face to face, so I got on stage and started screaming and squealing and twitching.

David Byrne •389

When the Heads started speaking French, The Ramones plunged to the depths of misery and horror.

Tom Verlaine on an uneasy touring bus shared by The Ramones and Talking Heads •390

I think you have a duty to perform, you have to entertain people. But just 'cos someone might wear a sequinned jacket onstage does not mean that they are instantly interesting to watch.

Jarvis Cocker •391

With Dire Straits, it was so damn big. You're a part of a travelling circus. The lighting rig came from *Star Trek*. When we got to the point of carrying around our own stage, I decided I had had enough.

Mark Knopfler 2000 •392

On stage, I make love to 25,000 different people, then I go home alone.

Janis Joplin •393

It's not the first time I have died in Coventry.

Former Fairport Convention violinist Dave Swarbrick after reading his obituary in *The Daily Telegraph* •394

Usually, when we come off stage, there are people waiting with towels, drinks... Here, I fell over and no one gave a toss.

Spandau Ballet's Gary Kemp on Live Aid •395

We did this show with Nirvana at the Warfield in San Francisco. They plugged in and from the first chord, Kurt flew into the audience. He was surfing the crowd while playing the song. The crowd threw him back onto the stage, and he hit the first line of the vocal. I was like, 'Fuck it, there is no way we can beat that'. Thurston Moore of Sonic Youth, 1994 •396

Most of the time you really don't know where you are. It's very possible that you may come out on stage and say, 'It's great to be here in St. Louis' and you could very well be in Denver or Seattle. That's happened.

Tom Waits 1985 •397

One pill makes you larger

And one pill makes you small
And the ones that mother gives you
Don't do anything at all.

Go ask Alice

When she's
ten feet
tall.

Jefferson Airplane *White Rabbit* (1967)
from the album *Surrealistic Pillow* •398

11 WHITE RABBIT

My advice to people today is as follows: if you take the game of life seriously, if you take your nervous system seriously, if you take your sense organs seriously, if you take the energy process seriously, you must turn on, tune in, and drop out.

Timothy Leary 1966, published in *The Politics of Ecstasy* •399

As far as I can see, the history of experimental art in the twentieth century is intimately bound up with the experience of intoxication.

Will Self *The Face*, 1994 •400

If you remember the 1960s, you weren't there. George Harrison •401

I had taken some strong psychedelics right before I went on stage. I was struggling to keep myself grounded. My guitar was like rubber.

Carlos Santana of the Woodstock experience •402

She goes running for the shelter
Of her mother's little helper,
And it helps her on her way
Gets her through her busy day.

Rolling Stones *Mother's Little Helper*
(Jagger & Richards), (1966) from the album *Aftermath* •403

I did some good writing, I think, on cocaine...
Song For Sharon – but it kills your heart, takes
all your energy, puts it up in your brain, gives
you the arrogance that, you know, ruined
Jaco Pastorius. I watched it ruin a lot of people.

Joni Mitchell 1988 •404

I got registered as an addict, which is really the first step to getting
out. Because the first thing you have to do is admit you're on the stuff,
which you tend not to do. I spent at least three years   pretending I
wasn't a junkie, that I didn't really 'need' heroin.
Which is nonsense. And when you have to go to a clinic
every day to pick it up, along with all the other
junkies, then you know.

Marianne Faithfull 1978 •405

Nobody stopped thinking about those psychedelic
experiences. Once you've been to some of those
places, you think, 'How can I get back there
again but make it a little easier on myself.'

Jerry Garcia of The Grateful Dead, *Rolling Stone*, 01989 •406

Going into rehab became a habit,
something to break the boredom,
like cigarettes. When things got
bad at home I'd get raging drunk,
pass out and then spend ten days
in rehab. Ronnie Spector •407

It's not what isn't, it's
what you wish was that
makes unhappiness...I
think I think too much,
that's why I drink.

Janis Joplin •408

I never get drunk. Two drinks and I get a headache and fall asleep. Lou Reed •409

I think the biggest misconception about me is that I'm a moron, a drunk who can't put my trousers on.
Shane MacGowan ex-Pogues 1995 •410

It's ridiculous. Some people still see us as a drunken novelty act even after four albums and seven years and Christ knows how many successful tours.
Spider Stacy
of The Pogues •411

For somebody who burnt the candle at both ends, Shane's doing pretty well to still be around. He's never really made a go at cleaning himself up, let's hope he does soon. He's been on holiday in Greece, and is looking a lot healthier.
Darryl Hunt of The Pogues, 1991 •412

I was happy in the haze of a drunken hour, But heaven knows I'm miserable now.
The Smiths *Heaven Knows I'm Miserable Now*
(Morrissey/Johnny Marr) (1984) from the album
The Smiths •413

I'm a total beer slob. Sheryl Crow •414

What's the point of going to college if you can't drink beer?

John Homme of Queens Of The Stone Age, 2000 •415

I was looking for some action,
But all I found was cigarettes and alcohol.

Oasis *Cigarettes and Alcohol* (1994) from the album *Definitely Maybe* •416

The replacements gave me a new respect for drinking. They took drinking a lot to this new art form level – not about being a total idiot, but about being this beautiful perfect drunk. Billie Joe Armstrong of Green Day 1996 •417

Sex and drugs and rock and roll
Is all my brain and body need.
Sex and drugs and rock and roll
Is very good indeed.

Ian Dury *Sex and Drugs and Rock and Roll,* (with Chas Jankel) (1976); from the album *Sex and Drugs and Rock and Roll* •418

If I had my way I would have sex, drugs and rock and roll at least four to six hours a day.

Perry Farrell of Jane's Addition, circa 1993 •419

I spent most of the Eighties, most of my life, riding around in somebody else's car, in possession of, or ingested of, something illegal, on my way from something illegal to something illegal with many illegal things happening all around me. Iggy Pop *The Guardian,* 1996 •420

I can honestly say, all the bad things that ever happened to me were directly attributed to drugs and alcohol. I mean, I would never urinate at the Alamo at nine o'clock in the morning dressed in a woman's evening dress sober. Ozzy Osbourne 1992 •421

Everything I've ever loved was immoral, illegal or grew hair on your palms.

Steven Tyler of Aerosmith •422

It details how she started out as a prostitute, got addicted to heroin, and eventually became a successful singer. And if you read it backwards, it doubles as a biography of Courtney Love.

Mark Lamarr on a biography of Billie Holliday •423

Kids, don't buy drugs. Wait until you're a rock star and they give them to you free.

Bill Nighy as Billy Mack *Love Actually,* 2003 •424

Ecstasy is a drug so strong it makes white people think they can dance. Lenny Henry •425

Think of what you could do with all the money they spend trying to fight drugs. Legalize them. Take the profit and the glamour out of them. Lou Reed 1989 •426

Mushrooms make me too fucking giggly. I just laugh at everything. I don't like to laugh too much.

Eminem 2000 •427

Summer breeze makes me feel fine Blowing through the jasmine in my mind.

Isley Brothers *Summer Breeze* (1973) •428

My first drug experience was sniffing glue. We tried it, and moved on to Carbona. That's why we wrote songs about it. It was a good high, but it gave you a bad high. I guess it destroys your brain cells. Johnny Ramone 2001 •429

I'll never stop smoking pot. I'm a drug addict and always fucking will be. I like my pot.

Shaun Ryder of The Happy Mondays 1991 •430

Follow her down to a bridge by a fountain
Where rocking horse people eat marshmallow pies.
Everyone smiles as you drift past the flowers
That grow so incredibly high.

The Beatles *Lucy In The Sky With Diamonds*, (Lennon & McCartney) (1967) from the album *Sgt. Pepper's Lonely Hearts Club Band* •431

When I found drugs, I thought I'd found the greatest thing. All you do is snort this shit up your nose or stick this needle in your arm, and you're a fucking genius.

Flea of The Red Hot Chili Peppers 1995 •432

I heard that your brain stops growing when you start doing drugs. Let's see, I guess that makes me 19.

Steven Tyler of Aerosmith, 1979 •433

I've never had problems with drugs. I've had problems with the police.
Mick Jagger of Rolling Stones 1999 •434

I've got no time for drugs any more... I tried them all and wouldn't recommend any of them.
Mick Jagger •435

From there my
Life went downwards
Like walking down hills
'Cos what ruined my life
Was drugs and pills
It's not worth smoking
Or doing drugs
'Cos if you're gonna do it,
You'll be with thugs

Eminem *Guilty Conscience* (1999)
from the *Slim Shady LP* •436

I felt in retrospect that
getting rid of the drugs allowed
the real problems to surface. It
allowed light to come into a lot of
dark corners, and then you had to
deal with the real issues that the
drugs had just been covering up.
That's a process of several years.

Roseanne Cash •437

All I can say is that drugs are
a retreat. Artistic people are
by nature so volatile, and if
you're highly strung, which
I am, you're vulnerable.

Boy George 1989 •438

My heart is broke, But I have some glue Help me inhale, And mend it with you.
Nirvana *Dumb* (1993) from the album *In Utero* •439

WHITE RABBIT

Slugs and snails are after me,
DDT keeps me happy.
Now I guess I'll have to tell 'em,
That I got no cerebellum

The Ramones *Teenage Lobotomy* (1977)
from the album *Rocket To Russia* •440

In the case of heroin, the drug's failure for Eric was not
to live up to his expectations in helping to create some
work of genius, or help him towards some profound
recognition of life. Ray Coleman on Eric Clapton, 1985 •441

It makes me feel like a fly with its wings stuck in honey.

Captain Beefheart on dope •442

What will we do there?
We'll get high.
What will we touch there?
We'll touch the sky.
But why the tears then?
I'll tell you why –
It's all too beautiful.

Small Faces
Itchycoo Park
(1967) •443

How I got to be a psychedelic guru was I just appointed myself one. Basically, all you have to do to become one is take enough drugs.

Lux Interior of The Cramps, 1980 •444

Nicotine, Valium, Vicodin, Marijuana, Ecstasy and Alcohol, C-c-c-c-c-cocaine.

Queens of the Stone Age
Feel Good Hit of the Summer, (2000) from the album *R* •445

PUBLIC IMAGE

You never listened to a word that I said
Or did the interest go so much deeper?
It must have been the colour of my hair.

P.I.L. *Public Image* (words: John Lydon)
(1978) from the album *Public Image* •446

12

Style's not something that you decide on on Monday and photograph on Thursday. You've been developing that for your whole life.

Simon Le Bon •447

For a start, the band is much more handsome since I joined.

Sid Vicious •448

What was so good about the 60s was that we have so many great dressers to copy. Every time I saw Brian Jones with some new trousers I had to get some. Patti Smith •449

Punk was just a way to sell trousers.

Malcolm McLaren •450

I remember standing in front of the stage waiting for them to come on, and McLaren coming down the stairs with Vivienne Westwood, and she was wearing the first bondage suit I'd ever seen. And I thought, 'fucking hell! What is that?' It was quite striking.

Pat Collier of The Vibrators on a 100 Club gig •451

I got a pair of salmon pink jeans and ran 'em up on my mum's sewing machine. They used to stop traffic.

Pete Shelley of The Buzzcocks •452

When we started we wanted some kind of definite anti-glitter look, 'cos that what was going on then. It's amazing how they've changed punk rock bands into glitter. I mean these clothing stores that sold glitter stuff are now selling the same stuff, but now it's punk fashions. Johnny Ramone •453

Of course we are big fans of Roxy Music. Inside the first album, Roxy Music, you learn what a really cool 70s rock and roll outfit means. Platform boots, tight jacket. Wahoo! Jean-Benoit Dunckel of Air 2001 •454

I mean, in a couple of years time, I'll probably look at a picture of me in platforms and say, 'What the hell was I doing?' Elton John 1973 •455

In England, glamour's in the gutter, it's everywhere, anywhere you want to find it. Boy George Smash Hits, 1982 •456

Boy George is all England needs – another queen who can't dress.
Joan Rivers •457

I'd like the band to be remembered as a good band, not as a funny old drag queen in a hat with some silly pop songs. Boy George on Culture Club •458

I like a suit but I don't look right in a suit. I put a suit on, my face just don't go with the suit, man. My face – I just ain't got a suit face. It's too bumpy. Weird.

Bruce Springsteen 1975 •459

Bryan Ferry is the only popular music star to have mastered the visual grammar of Jermyn Street, the only one ever to have worn a real tweed jacket.

Peter York •460

My relationship with rock and roll is like Lenny Bruce's with modern jazz – I like the clothes and the attitude.

John Cooper Clarke •461

She looks like she don't know better.
A case of partial extreme.
Dressed in a Robert Hall sweater.
Acting like a soap opera queen...

Blondie Rip Her To Shreds, (1977) from the album Blondie •462

I have to be honest – the first time I saw Cher, I thought she was a hooker.

Ronnie Spector •463

A certain amount of uplift and control, just what a bouncing boy needs when dressed in tights on stage.

Ian Anderson justifies his codpiece •464

I'm a size queen right? Honestly, I am, I can't lie. My friends sometimes say, 'you know, Janet, its not always about the size, but the magic in the wand.' And I'm like, 'but there's nothing wrong with a big magic wand.'

Janet Jackson 2001 •465

Let's face it, if I was a dentist it wouldn't be quite the same. If there are uglier guys around I don't know where they are, and yet I am the King of Pussy!

Gene Simmons •466

Chicks all dig the Wolf. They all dig the Wolf. Because he is a mighty wolf, he's a mountain wolf, he wipes out his tracks.

Howlin' Wolf obviously disputes Gene's claim •467

Cutie the bomb
Met her at a beauty salon
With a baby Louis Vuitton
Under her underarm.

Kanye West *Gold Digger* (2005)
from the album *Late Registration* •468

It was huge. At that time, it was the reason I did everything. It's the reason I played the guitar – because of my nose. The reason I write songs was because of my nose.

Pete Townshend 1968 •469

David Byrne would qualify as an artist. I mean, by appearance's sake. He looks like he's dying.

David Lee Roth •470

I know I look ridiculous sometimes, absolutely idiotic, but remember, when I started out I was quite rotund.

Elton John 1976 •471

Elvis Costello is terrible, all fat and sweaty. Can't dance either.

Ian McCulloch •472

I don't want to be one of those middle-aged guys who turns up with the baseball hat on the wrong way round.

Elvis Costello •473

What he's doing is what I desperately wanted to do, which is to age with dignity in this business.

Pete Townshend on Eric Clapton, 1985 •474

I'd hate to go down in history as the man who spawned a thousand Goth bands. Nick Cave •475

I always had denied I was a Goth. Then again, looking back on titles like *Sacrilege* and *Serpent's Kiss*, I guess the weight of evidence is against me.

Wayne Hussey of The Mission •476

All you Goths can fuck off back to your tents. The Mission aren't on 'till tomorrow.

Bernard Sumner of New Order 2001 •477

We use white light – coloured lights are for Christmas trees.

Peter Murphy of Bauhaus •478

It's my life and my body, and if I want to fuck myself up and have a beard and wear my hair long, that's my business. Elvis Costello 1991 •479

Long hair is an unpardonable offence which should be punishable by death.

Morrissey •480

Sally's gotta wig,
Ricky's gotta wig,
Baby's gotta wig,
Kate's gotta wig.
Fred's gotta cheap toupee,
Keith's gotta big bouffant on.

The B-52's *Wig,* (1987) from the album *Bouncing Off The Satellite* •481

I had black hair so people said we were goth. Now I have red hair so people say we're glam.

Marilyn Manson 1998 •482

Blonde is just a state of mind. You definitely have more fun.
I've been so popular since I dyed my hair. Lou Reed 1974 •483

Once I went blonde, there was no turning back. And when
the roots began to show, I just got too lazy to deal with it,
and people loved it even more. Debbie Harry 1977 •484

Paul Weller just stole everything. He's a skinny twat who has the worst haircut going. Ian McCulloch •485

I was a skinhead years ago. This was
before punk and just after mods. I was
15. Then I became a 'Suedehead' because
I grew my hair some. After that I was a
'casual,' which meant your hair was longer
still. Everything was defined by your hair.

Bernard Sumner of New Order 1993 •486

If Britney Spears would paint her ass green,
I'm sure you could spot green asses all over
LA. As soon as the word was out.
Billie Joe Armstrong of Green Day 2000 •487

I don't see why there has to be an age limit to performing rap. There's no age limit in rock — for fuck's sake look at Kiss!

Ice-T •488

13

**Why is the bedroom so cold, turned away on your side?
Is my timing that flawed, our respect run so dry?**

Joy Division *Love Will Tear Us Apart* (1980)
from the album *Unknown Pleasures* •489

I met her at the Burger King, we fell in love by the soda machine,
So we took the car downtown, the kids were hanging out all around.
Then we went down to Coney Island; on the coaster and around again,
And no one's gonna ever tear us apart, 'cause she's my sweetheart.

Ramones *Oh Oh I Love her So,* (1977) from the album *Leave Home* •490

I love romance! I love being treated like a princess. I think all women should be.

Kylie 2001 •491

People carry roses,
Make promises by the hours,
My love she laughs like the flowers,
Valentines can't buy her.

Bob Dylan *Love Minus Zero/No Limit* (1965) from the album *Bringing it All Back Home* •492

Whenever I'm alone with you
You make me feel like I am home again.
Whenever I'm alone with you
You make me feel like I am whole again.

The Cure *Lovesong* (1989) from the album *Disintegration* •493

Well it ain't no secret
I've been around a time or two.
Well I don't know baby maybe
  you've been around too.
Well there's another dance
All you gotta do is say yes
And if you're rough and ready for love
Honey I'm tougher than the rest.

Bruce Springsteen

Tougher Than The Rest (1987)
from the album *Tunnel Of Love* •494

Juliet, when we made love you used to cry
You said I love you like the stars above,
I'll love you 'til I die.

Dire Straits

Romeo and Juliet (Mark Knopfler), (1981)
from the album *Making Movies* •495

Only love can make it rain
The way the beach is kissed by the sea
Only love can make it rain
Like the sweat of lovers laying in the field.

The Who *Love Reign O'er Me* (Townshend) (1973)
from the album *Quadrophenia* •496

I said I'm strong, straight, willing
To be a shelter in a storm
Your willow, oh willow – when the sun is out.

Joan Armatrading *Willow* (1977) from the album *Show Some Emotion* •497

The amusement park rises bold and stark
Kids are huddled on the beach in a mist
I wanna die with you Wendy on the streets tonight
In an everlasting kiss.

Bruce Springsteen *Born To Run* (1975)
from the album *Born To Run* •498

I found my love by the gasworks crofts
Dreamed a dream by the old canal,
Kissed my girl by the factory wall
Dirty old town, dirty old town.

Ewan MacColl *Dirty Old Town* (1950) •499

Just a perfect day.
You made me forget myself.
I thought I was someone else,
Someone good.

Lou Reed *Perfect Day* (1973)
from the album *Transformer* •500

Somewhere in her smile she knows
That I don't need no other lover
Something in her style that shows me,
I don't want to leave her now
You know I believe and how.

The Beatles *Something* (Harrison) (1969)
from the album *Abbey Road* •501

To me he was Earth,
and I rooted in his soil.
I to he was Sky vast and free
of the burden from which he toiled.

Cowboy Junkies *To Love
Is To Bury* (1993) from the album
The Trinity Sessions •502

But blood and fire are too much for these restless arms to hold,
and my nights of desire they're calling me back to your fold.
And I am calling you, calling you from 10,000 miles away.
Won't you whet my fire with your love?

Indigo Girls *Blood and Fire* (Ray/Saliers) (1989)
from the album *Indigo Girls* •503

Adolescents tend to be passionate people, and passion is no less real because it is directed towards a hot-rod, a commercialised popular singer, or the leader of a black-jacketed gang.

Canadian educationist and sociologist Edgar Z Friedenberg 1959 •504

At 13 I thought I was in love with this guy,
Anytime I caught his eye I thought that I'd just die.

Ms Dynamite *Dy-na-my-tee* (2002) from the album
A Little Deeper •505

I can hold a thunderhead in my heart,
And in my bed I can dream a winter's gale
And wake up drenched
A stormy pale.

Laura Veirs *Icebound Stream* (2004)
from the album *Carbon Glacier* •506

**Baby, sweet baby, you're my drug
Come on and let me taste your stuff.
Baby, sweet baby, bring me your gift
What surprise you gonna hit me with?**

Lucinda Williams *Essence* (2001)
from the album *Essence* •508

When you gonna make
   up your mind
When you gonna love you
   as much as I do?

Tori Amos *Winter* (1991) from
the album *Little Earthquakes* •507

Touch if u will my stomach
Feel how it trembles inside.
You've got the butterflies all tied up.

Prince *When Doves Cry* (1984)
from the album *Purple Rain* •509

There's a club, if you'd like to go,
You could meet somebody who really loves you.
So you go, and you stand on your own,
And you leave on your own,
And you go home,
And you cry,
And you want to die.

The Smiths *How Soon Is Now?,* (words: Morrissey)
(1985) from the album *Meat Is Murder* •510

I would change for you but babe that doesn't mean I'm gonna be a better man,
Give the ocean what I took from you so one day you could find it in the sand
And hold it in your arms again.

Crooked Fingers *Sleep All Summer* (Eric Bachmann) (2004)
from the album *Diginity And Shame* •511

The Stone Roses album, I really like it, but it's all singing about she this and she that... never write songs about girls.

Ian McCulloch •512

See I reckon you're about an 8 or a 9,
Maybe even 9 and a half in four beers time.
That blue Topshop top you've got on IS nice,
Bit too much fake tan though – but yeah you score high.

Streets *Fit But You Know It* (2004) from the album *A Grand Don't Come For Free* •513

I fancy this, I fancy that,
I wanna be so flash,
I give a little muscle
And spend a little cash.
But all I get is bitter and a nasty little rash.

Squeeze *Cool For Cats* (1979) from the album *Cool For Cats* •514

Guys would sleep with a bicycle if it had the right colour lip gloss on. They have no shame. They're like bull elks in a field. Tori Amos •515

Girls run around with no clothes on,
To borrow a pound for a condom.
If it wasn't for chip fat they'd be frozen –
They're not very sensible.

Kaiser Chiefs *I Predict A Riot* (2005) from the album *Employment* •516

I didn't lose my virginity until I was 18. The first time was a nightmare. Who shows you how to use a condom?

Adam Ant •517

If I was a girl, I'd rather fuck a rock star than a plumber.

Gene Simmons of Kiss, circa 1986 •518

You get used to being a sex god.

Dave Gedge of The Wedding Present 1992 •519

I got a pair of red, synthetic satin women's pants through the post the other day with a phone number on. That was quite strange. I haven't tried the phone number. In times of stress I may. Jarvis Cocker •520

I'm the only genuine sex symbol in the current pop scene.

So said Ian McCulloch in the 1980s •521

I thought everybody in rock had illegitimate children.

Rod Stewart •522

I think Mick Jagger would be astounded and amazed if he realised to how many people he is not a sex symbol.

Angie Bowie •523

As far as I'm concerned, the benefit
of being a black Irishman is that I pull
more chicks. Phil Lynott Thin Lizzy •524

During the war time an American pilot,
Made every air raid a time of excitement.

Squeeze *Labelled With Love* (1981) from the
album *East Side Story* •525

I'm very healthy and natural when
it comes to sex. Strange locations
always turn me on. Aeroplane toilets.
I think that would turn anybody on.

Bjork 1996 •526

In our minds, love and lust are really separated. It's hard to
find someone that can be kind and you can trust enough to
leave your kids with, and isn't afraid to throw her man up
against the wall and lick him from head to toe. Tori Amos •527

For me, rock and roll is all about when you're in a bar and
you're in love with someone and you want to fuck them
and a band's playing. Mark Eitzel of American Music Club 1994 •528

Anything can be sex. Getting off is sex. Getting
to an audience is sex. Looking is sex. Your
body is a framework with infinite possibilities.

Lou Reed 1975 •529

She can make U crazy if U're 2 close 2 her heat
She can make U sad when U're happy as can be
She can make U shoot your ego all over your sheets
All is hers in love and war, my little Scarlet Pussy.

Prince *Scarlet Pussy,* 1988 •530

It all stems from Nico actually. She was the one
who took me when I was a skinny little naive brat
and taught me how to eat pussy and all about the
best French wines and German champagnes.

Iggy Pop •531

I prefer snogging and petting to full sex
– it leaves more to the imagination.

Jarvis Cocker of Pulp 1995 •532

I've never taken advantage of one
night stands. It's like treating sex like
sneezing. Sex is a fairly disgusting
sort of tufted, smelly-area kind of
activity, which is too intimate to
engage in with strangers.

Thom Yorke of Radiohead 1995 •533

Sex? I'd rather have a cup of tea.

Boy George •534

Sometimes a woman can really persuade you to make an asshole of yourself.

Rod Stewart 2001 •535

You consider me the young apprentice
Caught between your Scylla and Charybdis.
Hypnotized by you if I should linger
Staring at the ring around your finger.

Police *Wrapped Around Your Finger* (1983)
from the album *Synchronicity* •536

Why'd ya do it, she said, when you know it makes me sore,
'Cause she had cobwebs up her fanny and I believe in giving to the poor.
Why'd ya do it, she said, why'd you spit on my snatch?
Are we out of love now, is this just a bad patch?

Marianne Faithfull *Why D'ya Do It?* (1979)
from the album *Broken English* •537

I know you won't believe it's true,
I only went with her 'cos she looks like you.

Pulp *Babies* (1994) from the album *His 'n' Hers* •538

The other night, this guy gave me head. I'm not gay. I don't think so, anyway. I don't know. I just wanted to see what it felt like. And you know, he stunk. I thought 'it's going to be good, because he's a guy.' He went at it like he was eating corn on the cob or something.

Perry Farrell of Jane's Addiction 1991 •539

I see myself as a bisexual man who's never had a homosexual experience.

Brett Anderson of Suede 1993 •540

If I decide to have sex with a man, I'm not sure that I absolutely have to be a gay role model.

Bob Mould of Sugar, ex-Husker Du 1994 •541

Them lot, I think they fancy me. I think they're all gay.

Liam Gallagher's eloquent appraisal of the press •542

Sure I love Liam – but not as much as I love Pot Noodles.

Noel Gallagher •543

There are 400 million sperm in each ejaculation – and if you look around, take a look at some people, it's kinda hard to imagine that they beat 400 million. It makes one wonder.

Tom Waits 1999 •544

I'll die as I stand here today
Knowing that deep in my heart
They'll fall to ruin one day
For making us part.

Pretenders *Back On The Chain Gang*
(words: Chrissie Hynde), 1982 •545

Maybe the most you can expect from a relationship that goes bad is to come out of it with a few good songs.

Marianne Faithfull on the disintegration of her relationship with Mick Jagger •546

Am I not pretty enough?
Is my heart too broken?
Do I cry too much?
Am I too outspoken?

Kasey Chambers *Not Pretty Enough* from the album
Barricades and Brick Walls •547

Into the boundary
Of each married man,
Sweet deceit comes calling
And negativity lands.

Elton John *Sacrifice* (words: Bernie Taupin) (1989)
from the album *Ice On Fire* •548

It's been seven hours and fifteen days,
Since you took your love away.
I go out every night and sleep all day,
Since you took your love away.

Sinead O'Connor *Nothing Compares 2 U*
(written by Prince) (1990) from the album
I Do Not Want What I Haven't Got •549

I was so struck by the fact that your heart does break.

Bob Geldof on breaking up with Paula Yates •550

Whenever you're near
I hide my tears
Behind a painted smile.

Isley Brothers *Behind A Painted Smile* (1969) •551

It's knowing that he knows you now after only guessing.
It's the thought of him undressing you or you undressing
I want you
He tossed some tattered compliment your way
And you were fool enough to love it when he said
I want you.

Elvis Costello *I Want You* (1986) from the album *Blood And Chocolate* •552

Sweetness, sweetness I was only joking,
When I said I'd like to smash every tooth
In your head.
Oh sweetness, sweetness, I was only joking
When I said by rights you should be
Bludgeoned in your bed.

The Smiths *Bigmouth Strikes Again,*
(words: Morrissey) (1986) from the album
The Queen Is Dead •553

Why did you send me roses? Save them for someone's death.
The love you have to offer is only baby's breath.

Pretenders *Baby's Breath* (words: Chrissie Hynde) (1999)
from the album *Viva El Amor* •554

Do you want me?
Should I leave?
I know you're always telling me,
That you love me,
Just sometimes I wonder
If I should believe.
Oh, I love you.
God, I love you.
I'd kill a dragon for you.
I'd die.

Sinead O'Connor *Troy* (1987) from
the album *The Lion And The Cobra* •555

Mama always told me save yourself
Spend a little time and find the right girl.
Then again don't end up on the shelf —
Logical advice gets you in a whirl.

Joe Jackson *It's Different For Girls* (1979)
from the album *I'm The Man* •556

14

So we're comin' out of the kitchen,
'Cause there's somethin' we forgot to say to you.
Sisters are doin' it for themselves.
Standin' on their own two feet.
And ringin' on their own bells.

`Eurythmics` *Sisters Are Doin' It For Themselves*
(1985) from the album *Be Yourself Tonight* •557

Feminists should be concerned about
the personalities in rock and roll because
they will be the primary means by which
young women get the feminist message.

`Camille Paglia` controversial cultural critic, 1995 •558

SISTERS ARE DOIN' IT FOR THEMSELVES

Women are going to be the
new Elvises. That's the only
place for rock 'n' roll to go.

`Debbie Harry` in prime Blondie days •559

She always had a great sense of humour about all the attention... she was (and is) a face for the ages. And a pretty good singer and songwriter as a bonus.
Mick Rock on Debbie Harry, 1984 •560

Debbie's persona, innocent yet sluttish, arrogant yet waif-like, was consciously rooted in America's most mystical of all sex objects. Philip Norman on Debbie Harry's deference to Marilyn •561

Sadly, Blondie will never be a star simply because she ain't good enough, but for the time being I hope she's having fun. Charles Shaar Murray makes a crap prediction in 1975 •562

No one has ever seen my legs, my ass, my tits. Even my fucking face I've hidden beneath my fringe. I'm the original yashmak rocker. Chrissie Hynde of The Pretenders •563

I'm chuffed. I have two fantastic kids and I don't have to work. I figure I've made a fuck of a lot of noise in my life, so now is my time to be quiet. My worst nightmare would be for me to go out there and for every cab driver to think they knew who I was. I don't know you and you don't know me. Great. Let's keep it simple and tidy. Chrissie Hynde in *Mojo*, 2006 •564

I'm really a band animal. I just have no interest whatsoever in Chrissie Hynde at all. And when I'm on stage I think my whole purpose for being there is to make the guitarist looked good. Chrissie Hynde 1990 •565

Back before the flood, when Patti Smith began caterwauling poetry above an electric guitar, she probably didn't realise she was clearing the path for legions of bad-tempered demoiselles with dark clothing and three-subject notebooks full of lousy poems.

Steve Anderson in *Village Voice*, 1982 •566

Patti Smith has an aura that'd probably show up under ultraviolet light. She can generate more intensity with a single movement of one hand than most rock performers can produce in an entire set.

Charles Shaar Murray •567

Baby was a black sheep. Baby was a whore.
You know she got big. Well, she's gonna get bigger.
Baby got a hand; got a finger on the trigger.
Baby, baby, baby is a rock-and-roll nigger.

Patti Smith *Rock'n'Roll Nigger* (1978) from the album *Easter* •568

We attract groupies of both sexes. The girls are far more forward in their suggestiveness.

Donita Sparks of L7 •569

My philosophy on life is that I'm not about my external appearance. What I have to say it's far more important than how long my eyelashes are.

Alanis Morissette •570

I recommend getting your heart trampled on to anyone
I recommend walking around naked in your living room.
Swallow it down (what a jagged little pill)
It feels so good (swimming in your stomach)

Alanis Morissette *You Learn* (1995) from
the album *Jagged Little Pill* •571

I don't mean that to be egotistical, but I'm
not writing fluff. I'm not writing for 8-year-olds.
I'm a woman and I'm a rock girl. **Meredith Brooks** •572

I created Punk for this day and age. Do you see Britney
walking around wearing ties and singing punk? Hell no.
That's what I do. I'm like a Sid Vicious for a new generation.

Avril Lavigne •573

When I was growing up I thought Kim Deal was the most brilliant woman in rock.

Shirley Manson on the Pixies'
bassist, 1996 •574

When I started, I got a lot
of attention because I was
aggressive, strident. People
liked that. **Shirley Manson**
of Garbage 1999 •575

I don't mean to be a diva, but some days
you wake up and you're Barbra Streisand.

Courtney Love •576

I don't want to do anything that's just straight glamorous.
It has to have some element of uneasiness or humour.

P.J. Harvey •577

I think people are always going to
think the worst of me. They're ready
and willing to cast me into these dark
holes, to say that I'm this physically
and mentally unstable character. So
I have to be careful not to present
them with such an easy target. P.J. Harvey
1997 •578

She sang like a rock 'n' roll
banshee and leapt about
the stage like a dervish. It
was the raunchiest, grittiest,
most attacking rhythm and
blues singing I'd ever heard.

Michael Thomas on Janis Joplin in *Ramparts*, 1967 •579

Janice could scream and squall just as hard as Tina, but Tina could dance. Janice couldn't. I couldn't. We weren't dancers. Tina is like a female James Brown. She is a mover and she looks good. Little Richard •580

Finally, she says, 'okay, Phil, one more time.' And she ripped her blouse off and grabbed the microphone, and she gave a performance that... I mean, your hair was standing on end. It was like the whole room exploded. I'll never forget that as long as I live, man. It was a magic moment.

Bob Krasnow on Tina Turner recording *River Deep, Mountain High*, with Phil Spector •581

When she came in, she was electric. We turned the lights down, just had a couple of sidelights on each wall. And she couldn't swing with the song with all her clothes on, so she took her blouse off and sang it just wearing a bra. What a body! It was unbelievable, the way she moved around.

Larry Levine recording engineer at the same session •582

In high school, Tina Turner always got straight A's for drama and gym. And she still getting them. Charles Shaar Murray •583

He'd lock the door, and then you knew you were gonna get it. One night in the studio he threw boiling hot coffee in my face. Said I wasn't singing the way he wanted, that I wasn't trying. Tina Turner on her abusive relationship with her husband Ike •584

She has a voice that was finally wasted in The Supremes, a voice with a kind of sleepy snarl in it, or else the pitch and faint breathlessness of a nervous girl singing for dimes. Dancing, she is like a wildly animated clothes-horse hung with quickly-changing gowns and silly hats. Philip Norman on Diana Ross •585

Aretha carries you back to church in everything that she does. Al Jackson on Aretha Franklin •586

You look at me and see the girl,
Who lives inside the golden world.
But don't believe that's all there is to see
You'll never know the real me.

Mariah Carey *Looking In* (1995) from the album *Daydreaming* •587

I could be more in control but I don't want to be. I'm always thirsty for surprise. Bjork •589

I'm not a raving loony. I'm a fiery, passionate woman who cares about what is happening in the world. Sinead O'Connor •588

I admire that, ...but I can't see myself doing it because I'm a loudmouthed cow. Charlotte Church after hearing that Celine Dion didn't speak for a whole day before a concert •590

I just do the same stuff I always did. I have a bigger apartment – that's the main change.
Norah Jones •591

Dolly Parton's just kind of a southern magnolia blossom that floats on the breeze. Linda Ronstadt •592

I'm not offended at all because I know I'm not a dumb blonde. I also know I'm not blonde.
Dolly Parton whips the rug from under her detractors' feet, 1993 •593

Most people say it would make a wonderful soap opera. I'm sure it could, but to me it's just my life. Tammy Wynette •594

I still think of myself as an awkward tomboy. It's something I'll never get over, no matter how many magazines I'm in. Jewel 1998 •595

I learned the truth at seventeen,
That love was meant for beauty queens,
And high school girls with clear skinned smiles,
Who married young and then retired.
Janis Ian *At Seventeen* (1975) from the album *Between The Lines* •596

A typical guy wants the woman under his thumb, like his housewife and all that, and we're not having it!
Ari Up lead singer of The Slits •597

Don't let anyone tell you that you have to be a certain way. Be unique. Be what you feel.

Melissa Etheridge •598

You don't have to be age 20 and size zero to be sexually viable or viable as a woman. Belinda Carlisle •599

I tell women, 'Go and masturbate! Get loads of kinky books and masturbate every day!' *They do* it from the age of nine. Björk *NME*, 1993 •600

I sometimes worry about using my lesbianism as a marketing tool. Let's get over it; it's my art now. k.d.lang •601

For a while, the genre seemed to be just about sex and crime. Rappers are storytellers; the stories don't need to be true!

Lauryn Hill •602

I'm not a big fan of Tracy Chapman but it's about time that a black woman is allowed to come across without having to wear a leather skirt where you can see her pubic hair sticking out.

Terence Trent D'Arby 1989 •603

'Girl' is not menstruating, 'Girl' is non-orgasmic, 'Girl' is naive, cute, bratty, unthreatening in her clumsiness and incompetence. 'Girl' is most of all, young. It is vanity in extremes. I have always called myself a girl, but I am going to stop now. Courtney Love of Hole, 1994 •604

The trouble with some women is that they get all excited about nothing – and then marry him. Cher •605

I was perceiving myself as good as a man or equal to a man and as powerful and I wanted to look ambiguous because I thought that was a very interesting statement to make through the media. Annie Lennox •606

Show me somebody that puts out an album every year and I'll show you a man who hasn't got two children and lives at home with them and has to get them up for school every morning. Oh God, what everyone needs in this business is a wife. It must be great. I wish I had a wife. Chrissie Hynde 1991 •607

MATERIAL GIRL

15

I am living in a material world,
And I am a material girl.
Madonna *Material Girl* (1995)
from the album *Like A Virgin* •608

I think I've always behaved
as if I were a star. Since I
was a kid I have behaved
as if somebody owed
me something.
Madonna 1990 •609

I'm sexy. How can
I avoid it? I'd have
to put a bag over
my head. But then
my voice would
come across. And
it's sexy. **Madonna** •611

I went to New York. I had a dream.
I wanted to be a big star. I didn't
know anybody. I wanted to dance.
I wanted to sing. I wanted to do
all those things. I wanted to make
people happy. I wanted to be
famous. I wanted everybody to
love me. I wanted to be a star.
I worked really hard and my dream
came true. **Madonna** on her
early aspirations •610

I sometimes think I was born to live up to my name. How could I be anything else but what I am, having been named Madonna? I would either have ended up a nun or this. Madonna 1992 •612

You can use the cage
I've got a lot of rope
No, I'm not full of rage,
I'm full of hope.
This is not a crime
and you're not on trial
Bend over, baby
I'm gonna make you smile
Madonna *Erotica* (1992)
from the album *Erotica* •613

Maybe I'm just a gay man inside a woman's body!

Madonna talking on Parkinson, 2005 •614

I think Madonna is particularly revolting. I find it hard to imagine why anyone would want to so cheapen themselves. The things she says are disgusting, and I'd kill anyone who used her kind of language around me.
Whitney Houston 1988 •615

Madonna is closer to organised prostitution than anything else. I mean, the music industry is obviously prostitution anyway, but there are degrees. Morrissey 1986 •616

I'm tough and I'm ambitious and I know exactly what I want. If that makes me a bitch – okay. Madonna •617

No one knows how to work this business like she does

Cher on Madonna •618

The thing about Madonna is that she is the ultimate consumer of pop culture.

Malcolm McLaren •619

Madonna is the speedboat, and the rest of us are just the Go-Go's on water skis

Liz Phair on Madonna •620

Madonna is more than a celebrity; she is the perfect hybrid that personifies the decadently greedy, selfish sexual decade that spawned her – a corporation in the form of flesh.

Kevin Sessum 1990 •621

You mean they don't realise I'm a songwriter as well as a slut?

Madonna 1989 •622

An entertainer is a whole different thing, an entertainer to me doesn't necessarily deal with reality. It's someone who makes you forget. It's like a drug, it's euphoric and I think it has its place in the world. But that's not the only thing I do. I think I'm an educator – and I do think I'm an artist.

Madonna •623

The result is *The Madonna Collection*, a collection of academic essays about Madonna that is alternately intriguing and infuriating. It's like watching a group of lecherous monks discuss a porn film in Latin.

Robert Worth in *The Guardian*, 1992 •624

I won't be happy until I'm as famous as God.

Madonna •625

16

POP

MUSIK!

New York, London, Paris, Munich,
Everybody talk about – Pop Musik!.

Pop Musik (1979) •626

A lot of pop music is about stealing pocket money from children.

Ian Anderson of Jethro Tull, *Rolling Stone,* 1989 •627

I'll grow old physically, but I won't grow old musically

Cliff Richard the Peter Pan of Pop •628

I'm just a normal, everyday kind of Goddess.

Sandie Shaw 1988 •629

In many ways I never felt like I fitted into all that L.A. lifestyle. I was too much of a fucking yob.

Rod Stewart •630

I love the fact that Rod's turned into such a twit – I can surprise people when I play his early 70's records.

Robert Elms on Rod Stewart's decline, *The Word,* 2006 •631

He was so mean it hurt him to go to the bathroom.

Britt Eklund about Rod Stewart •632

The worst part of being gay in the twentieth century is all that damn disco music to which one has to listen.

Quentin Crisp *Manners from Heaven,* 1984 •633

I love a good dance ditty. God, I love disco. I see no problem admiring the Bee Gees and being in The Sex Pistols.

Johnny Rotten 1998 •634

Barry White is the singer who turned black soul music into a product akin to soggy white blancmange. From Manila to Macclesfield his voice could be heard, grunting and gasping in a register of emotions from A to B flat, invariably expressing agitation at the prospect of imminent sexual intercourse and yet sounding as if somebody is throttling the vocalist with a pillow.

Philip Norman •635

Village People are about partying, a twinkle in the eye, and a bump in the groin.

Victor Willis •636

They didn't look like humans. They looked like foetuses. I felt physically ill when I saw them on TV.

The ever-restrained Julie Burchill on Bay City Rollers •637

Freddie was always a star. I remember him penniless years ago coming round to mine to bum a night's sleep on the floor – and he'd act like he was doing you a favour.

Queen's Roger Taylor 1974 •638

There was no way people were ever going to pay to see Benny and me performing.

Bjorn Ulvaeus Abba •639

We have to consider how we would look now compared to the memories people have of us.

Pop legends Abba explain why they turned down a £650 million offer to perform again •640

A bit of Elvis, a bit of Bolan, a bit of dub, a bit of rap, zap it through a satellite dish and away we go.

Tony James Sigue Sigue Sputnik •641

You don't always choose the fifteen minutes of fame that comes your way.

Hilary Lester Renee of Renee and Renato •642

All the bad publicity does toughen you up. The only way you can deal with the criticism is by learning not to care.

Simon Le Bon of Duran Duran •643

We had a strange paranoia that we'd be found out for the shallow charlatans we really were. We really weren't good enough to be adored by so many millions of people. Tom Bailey of The Thompson Twins. He's right •644

I lay a £100,000 bet with anyone, any journalist, that there'll be a point in my career when I win an Oscar in Hollywood. There's no doubt about it.

Wendy James of Transvision Vamp. Wish I'd taken the bet... •645

In the 18-year old wake of David Bowie's *Pin Ups,* few artists have been foolish enough to do a covers album. Duran Duran were the last notable culprits with 1995's inexplicable *Thank You*; and now Simple Minds have decided to come after them... Really, to call this a turkey would be unfair to the birds who share the name.

John Harris on Simple Minds' *Neon Lights;* in *Q magazine,* October 2001 •646

Jon was analytical; George intuitive. Jon was a bit of a lad; George was as camp as Christmas. And above all, George was the walking, talking, made up, dressed up living embodiment of London's underground nightlife. Jon thought the whole scene stank.

Dave Rimmer on the contrasting lead members of Culture Club •647

He was just starting out as a singer, he had the voice but not the control, really. He was really mad keen on rock music and the whole mythology of it. He loves it, and he really deserves to be where he is today, even though he was from Bromley and very middle class.

Rob Milne on Billy Idol •648

I wanted a name that would put us first in the phonebook – or second, if you count Abba.

Martin Fry ABC •649

The essence of pop is brilliant songs. The rest is sex, subversion, style and humour. Adam Ant •650

You don't have to be a great musician to make great records. You just have to have a lot of good ideas. Neneh Cherry •651

Wham! worked like crazy to make people think they were lazy. Behind the sun tans lay the sweat and toil of self-improvement. Dave Hill •652

When you start measuring your achievements by records sold and size of gigs you're in trouble. Bananarama sold more records than The Supremes, but are they better? Billy Bragg 1996 •653

It's maybe something you wouldn't want to be caught playing with the car windows down.
David 'Kid' Jensen on Chris De Burgh's *Lady In Red* •654

He's at his best when marching fearlessly into yawning canyons of schlock, epitomised by his all-time end-of-the-party smoocher *Three Times a Lady*. When Lionel sang it, dozens of couples threw their arms around each other's necks and began to sway clumsily, as if Richie had pressed some biological Go button.
Adam Sweeting on the effect of Lionel Richie at a 1992 Town & Country gig •655

The first concert I went to without my mom was Tears For Fears. I was probably 13. All I remember was that I smoked a whole pack of cigarettes and promptly threw up everywhere. Dido 2001 •656

I was a veteran, before I was a teenager.

Michael Jackson •657

I come before you less as an icon of pop and more as an icon of a generation.

Michael Jackson speaking at the Oxford Union •658

I don't look at it as he is not the hottest thing any more – I look at what he's done as a groundbreaking artist who opened a lot of doors for black acts. Michael Jackson is still amazing to me.

Missy Elliott •659

Michael is the wisest and at the same time most naive person I know.

Quincy Jones •660

Michael Jackson's album was only called 'Bad' because there wasn't enough room on the sleeve for 'Pathetic'. Prince •661

Love Sexy, it has to be said, is a turgid collection of inconclusive riffs and weak melodies, decorated to distraction by harsh and flashy ornamentation.

David Toop on Prince's album *Love Sexy,* in *The Sunday Times,* May 1988 •662

Bambi with testosterone.

Owen Gleiberman on Prince, in *Entertainment Weekly* •663

He looks like a dwarf who's been dipped in a bucket of pubic hair.

Boy George on Prince •664

Kylie is an enigma really. I think that's part of her power. She's actually the opposite of Madonna – Madonna, we feel we know everything about. Kylie, we feel we know nothing about.

Neil Tennant of the Pet Shop Boys, 2002 •665

I don't do anything to my backside. I work hard, I run around a lot and I dance when I have to. That's it.

Kylie on her fitness regime after those infamous *Spinning Around* gold hotpants, 2002 •666

Boredom is thy enemy! Change is as natural to me as breathing.

Kylie 2001 •667

I like seeing our records go up and Kylie and Phil Collins go down. There's no point moaning about it, you've got to get in there and stamp them out. Ian Brown of The Stone Roses 1990 •668

I loved Jordan. He was one of the greatest athletes of our time. Mariah Carey pays a moving tribute to... er... the King of Jordan •669

The Celine Dion we know and love is a handsome woman. That's not the way I remember her from Eurovision.

Surely Mr Wogan isn't suggesting a bit of nip and tuck? •670

Don't want to hear my favourite rapper doin' a love song. If I want to hear something soft, I'll throw on Luther Vandross. Ice Cube •671

I want our records to sell a million copies. I want to make as much money as Phil Collins.

William Reid of The Jesus and Mary Chain 1993 •672

Shania 'Oh I must remember to buy some mutton' Twain once performed at the Nobel Prize Peace Concert with Elton John and Phil Collins. You probably remember that year. They had to wrestle a Stanley knife off Nelson Mandela. Mark Lamarr •673

It's just like having all your fantasies come true – partying for a living.

Fat Boy Slim •674

I'm not interested in just being today's pop star. I want a career, like Stevie Wonder or Sting or Queen.

Jason Kay of Jamiroquai 1997 •675

A crippling affliction which leaves its victim unable to comprehend that no one actually likes them, despite overwhelming evidence to the contrary. Named after shamed dumper stalwart and ex Steps chipmunk Lisa Scott Lee, this terrifying disease seems to be spreading through the pop wilderness like wildfire leaving a number of has-beens desperately clinging onto the notion that they are still popular, despite sales evidence to prove otherwise. Even the dedicated staff at *The Dumper* have failed to find a cure, with Lisa Scott Lee herself still convinced that her natural home is in the upper echelons of the chart.

popjustice.com define 'Lisa Scott-Lee Disease'•676

Take That went to bed with coathangers in their mouths to wake up with smiles the next morning. East 17 went to bed with any young lady that was available to them.

Tom Watkins who managed both •677

The worst thing you can do is try and be cool. Honesty is the best policy – just be a dick and people respect you for it.

Robbie Williams •678

I show off – I'm a very good show off. It's what I do, it's what I'm good at.

Robbie Williams •679

When people come out of rehab, they usually go to secondary rehab for another six months and then enter back into society gradually. But I came out and did Top Of The Pops straight away!

Robbie Williams •680

I met Courtney Love and she said she'd like to sleep with me, but she couldn't cos of my 'pop-star thing'... so I said to her I couldn't sleep with her either – cos of her 'ugly thing'. Robbie Williams •681

When I first met him [David Beckham] I didn't know whether to shake his hand or lick his face.

Robbie Williams •682

Noel's run out of other people's ideas.

Robbie Williams on Oasis's Noel Gallagher•683

She's got a face like a satellite dish and ankles like my granny's.

Robbie Williams on British pop star Sophie Ellis Bextor •684

**We're the Spice Girls, yes indeed.
Just Girl Power is all we need.**

The Spice Girls master the art of rap in *Spice World:
The Movie* (1997) •685

**I don't think the Spice Girls are celebrated
as much as they should be. We championed
British pop worldwide. We toured everywhere
to sell-out crowds and I think there should
have been a reflection of that at February's
Brits anniversary.** Mel C •686

We're becoming Spice Women now.

Mel C on her new image •687

'Okay, girls, that was absolutely perfect without... really being any good at all.'

Jools Holland as the Spice Girls' musical director in their 1997 film *Spice World* •688

Becoming a solo singer is like going from an eau de toilette to a perfume. It's much more intense. **Geri Halliwell** •689

She's the ultimate wannabe self-made pop star, a pop dream. No matter where you live in the world or how well you can sing, you can still be a pop star. **John Robb** on the legacy of Geri Halliwell •690

Cowell: You sing like the Spice Girls.
Contestant: Thanks.
Cowell: Unfortunately, that wasn't a compliment.
From **Pop Idol** •691

I met someone the other night who's 28 years old, and he hasn't worked a day since he left college because he's pursuing a dream he'll never, ever realize: He thinks he's a great singer. Actually, he's crap. But nobody has said to him, 'Why have you been wasting your time for eight years?' **Simon Cowell** •692

The object of this competition is not to be mean to the losers but to find a winner. The process makes you mean because you get frustrated. Kids turn up unrehearsed, wearing the wrong clothes, singing out of tune and you can either say, 'Good job,' and patronize them or tell them the truth, and sometimes the truth is perceived as mean. Simon Cowell on *American Idol* •693

I thought Pop Idol was really disappointing and full of freaks and geeks and fatties. Marc Almond •694

Oooops, I did it again. After viewing the Britney Spears movie I can only say that my soul is damned, my legs are numb, and I am left with a buzzing sensation in the abdomen that I cannot explain. Now, first let it be said that it was a challenge to see the Britney movie, one that pitted movie reviewers in Kim Ute of sorts, except a lot less blood and a lot more inner turmoil. I can only assume that Mr Carrichner will attempt to claim that my 'love for Ms. Brit' has hardened my heart and that I only want to destroy this movie because I care so much. Let the record show that I have been bitter since 1986, way before Brit even hit the marketplace, so while I may have unresolved Tiffany issues, I am quite certain that there is no love lost between me and Britney. Steven J. Willett on Britney Spears in *Crossroads; at Rant 'n' Rave* (www.rantrave.com) •695

Where the hell is Australia anyway?

Britney Spears •696

I love seeing all my Mexican fans from the North.
Britney Spears •697

Britney would make a better prostitute than Christina. She's thicker. Snoop Dogg

on the relative merits of La Spears and L'Aguilera •698

You are surrounded by people, each one more false than the other, always ready to step on you. Either you quickly learn to survive or you fail, you lose everything as quickly as you find success. Christina Aguilera •699

Britney and I show a little tummy and it's like, 'Oh My God.' But N'Sync or Backstreet Boys will do repeated pelvic thrusts to an audience of pre-pubescent girls and nobody says anything!
Christina Aguilera •700

When popstars are 17 years old, the world and its pervy mother fancies them and says things like, 'Ooh I can't wait until they're 18 and I can get them bladdered down The Ram and do unspeakable acts to them'. Then the candles are blown out, the 18th birthday balloon pops and everyone realises they don't want to see said popstar's norks now they're 18 because it's all a bit 'sick'. See A-Teens, S Club Juniors, Charlotte Church, Richard Fleischeman
popjustice.com explain the '17 year old itch' phenomenon •701

Oh dear, oh dear. Second-rate teeny acts (Samantha Mumba, a1, S Club 7) or people who promised never to trouble us again (Lulu, Lisa Stansfield, Yazz, Erasure) sing Motown songs badly. And what on earth the admirable Chris Rea – neither second-rate nor teen fodder – is doing here is something he should be discussing with his advisors right now; as he sacks them.

John Aizlewood on *Motown Mania,* by various artists, in *Q magazine,* March 2001 •702

I had my first snog with a boy under an electricity pylon. Which is quite dangerous, really. So don't do that, kids.

Jenny Frost of Atomic Kitten dispenses sage advice to the young •703

Me? An angel! Just ask my mum about that!

'Voice of an Angel' singer Charlotte Church on the limits of her angelic status •704

Everyone says I'm like the girl next door... Y'all must have really weird neighbours!

Kelly Clarkson •705

I'd die if I was Madonna. I'd die. God, what a horrible way to live. And Michael Jackson! To be so famous and to feel so isolated. I feel so bad for them. I don't know how it feels, and I hope it never happens to me.

Hollywood actress Alicia Silverstone •706

I did not watch the Brit Awards on television last night. Recent experience suggests that such back-slap-athons are hazardous to my blood pressure. Indeed, simply reading about the Brits was quite enough to send me into a state of foaming apoplexy. Kylie, Dido, Travis, Westlife, S Club 7, Shaggy… and, topping it all off, Sting, emperor of wine-bar muzak. It was a line-up to make you howl, or at least despair of pop ever meaning anything, well, meaningful again…

Chart pop has become so redundant, so musically bankrupt, that the best we can do is collude with the mass delusion that a pocket-sized Oz automaton is a spunky sex goddess with a flawless sense of irony. I refer, of course, to Ms Minogue, whose numbingly formulaic 'Can't Get You Out of My Head' is being hailed as some work of postmodern electro-pop genius… In the new global celebrity culture, pop literally means nothing other than fame.

Barney Hoskyns
Editorial Director of *Rock's Backpages*
(www.rocksbackpages.com) in
The Independent, February 2002 •707

17

And the more I see – the more I know
The more I know – the less I understand.
I'm the changingman.

Paul Weller *Changing Man* (1995)
from the album *Stanley Road* •708

THE CHANGING MAN

Sometimes I don't
feel as if I am a
person at all. I'm
just a collection of
other people's ideas.
David Bowie •709

He was the
Scarlet Pimpernel
in fabulous drag.
Mick Rock on Bowie •710

I love girls. They're smashin'.
They're as good as blokes.
David Bowie 1972 •711

None of us exist. We're in the Twilight Zone. We'll all go to hell, 'cause we set ourselves up as Gods.

David Bowie 1972 •712

It's a movie that is so corrupt with a script that is so devious and insidious. It is the scariest movie ever written. You feel a total victim there, and you know someone's got the strings on you.

David Bowie talking about Los Angeles •713

Rock stars have taken over from the fake prophets of Jesus' time, spreading a phoney religion and getting paid for it.

David Bowie 1973 •714

I'm one of the world's actors, in the broadest sense of the word. I'm an exhibitionist. I like showing off. I'm a peacock.

David Bowie 1973 •715

It is Bowie, perhaps more than any other performer, who began the tyranny of style, image and media manipulation which has been the theme of pop music for the past ten years. Mick Brown •716

The first time I saw Ziggy Stardust it bowled me over. I was a journalist at the time, but that's when I decided I wanted to write songs and perform. Steve Harley 1974 •717

He is so dominating the teenage culture not only because he knows so many more things than his rivals, but because he understands how to exploit them to stay ahead, if only instinctively. Michael Watts 1976 •718

I have to pick a city with friction in it. It has to be a city that I don't know how it works. I've got to be at odds with it. As soon as I feel comfortable, I can't write in it any more.
David Bowie 1979 •719

He also provided the impetus for kids to dye their hair fantasy colours like blue, green, scarlet and purple – colours that human hair has never achieved unaided – to wear clothes based on *Flash Gordon* comics and 30s movies, to be exactly what they wanted to be and screw reality, Jack! Charles Shaar Murray •720

I had no melody, so I only sang the lines I'd written for five bars at a time. Having sung one line, I'd take a breath and do the same thing again, and so on to the end. I never knew the complete melody until I'd finished the song and played the whole the whole thing back.
David Bowie on *"Heroes"* •721

He said 'Can I change the lyrics?' I said,
'Of course, you're David Bowie; I live with
my mother. Of course you can change the lyrics.'
Luther Vandross on his collaboration with David Bowie •722

I feel like an actor when I'm onstage, not a rock artist.
It's not much of a vocation, being a rock and roller.
David Bowie •723

I once asked John Lennon what
he thought of what I do. He said,
'It's great, but it's just rock and roll
with lipstick on.' David Bowie 1999 •724

I've been disappointed with some of
my work, but I do like an awful lot
of it, I'm afraid. My one problem
is that I'm not very consistent.
David Bowie 1999 •725

THANK YOU FOR THE MUSIC 18

But I have a talent, a wonderful thing
'cause everyone listens when I start to sing.

Abba *Thank You For The Music* (1983) from
the album *Thank You For The Music* •726

Music is your own experience, your own thoughts, your wisdom. If you don't live it, it won't come out of your horn. They teach you there's a boundary line to music. But, man, there's no boundary line to art. Charlie Parker 1955 •727

Life is like the car, and your art, or whatever you produce, is the caravan. As long as the car's in front of the caravan you can go places. The other way around, you're not going anywhere.

Jarvis Cocker 2001 •728

A lot our lyrics were obscure but not unintelligent ...thoughtful gibberish.

Ian McCulloch of Echo & The Bunnymen •729

It's like a novelist writing far out things. If it makes a point and makes sense, then people like to read that. But if it's off in left field and goes over the edge, you lose it. The same with musical talent, I think.

Johnny Cash •730

An artist's duty is rather to stay open-minded and in a state where he can receive information and inspiration. You always have to be ready for that little artistic Epiphany. Nick Cave •731

Rock 'n' roll, man, it changed my life. It was like the Voice of America, the real America coming into your home. It was the liberating thing, the out. Once I had the guitar, I had the key to the highway. Bruce Springsteen 1978 •732

The message in the records is, just follow your heart, as corny as that may sound. There are people trying to hold onto the things they believe in, but it's all very difficult.
Bruce Springsteen 1978 •733

What's wrong with sentimental? Sentimental means you love, you care, you like stuff. The thing is, we're frightened to be sentimental. Paul McCartney 1983 •734

I like a spirituality with a God that knows how to take his girl to the dance club, dance all night, have a little drink, kiss the kid when they come back in and go to sleep. God doesn't need a chauffeur. Jeff Buckley 1994 •735

My idea of heaven is a place where the Tyne meets the Delta, where folk music meets the blues. Mark Knopfler *Mojo*, 1986 •736

I am a perfectionist. Some even claim that I'm a terror, a dictator and they're right. But I'm also talented and I know when I create something great. Lou Reed 1998 •737

Rebellion, love, hate, sex, denial: all these will still be here when we're done. I like to stick to the old standbys in my songs. Paul Westerberg ex-The Replacements 1993 •738

That's why I do this music business thing, it's communication with people without having the extreme inconvenience of actually phoning anybody up. Morrissey •739

Immortality doesn't bother me. If people have forgotten about *I Don't Like Mondays* two weeks from now, no problem. Bob Geldof 1979 •740

Everyone goes on about the idea of the sensitive artist, but for me that's all bollocks. I can't stand the idea of being a sad, lonely bedside poet I'd much rather be perceived as loud and arrogant. Damon Albarn of Blur 1997 •741

It's always a Catch-22 situation. They hate you if you're the same, and they hate you if you're different. Eddie Van Halen •742

Artists everywhere steal mercilessly all the time and I think this is healthy.

Peter Gabriel 1992 •743

I'm not plagued, I'm strictly a loner. I don't have any friends. I like to be on my own best of all. Scott Walker

Melody Maker, 1966 •744

People sometimes ask me if I'm happy, and I tell them to fuck off.

Thom Yorke of Radiohead 1995 •745

I hate art. I can't stand it. It's treating something that's supposed to be good as precious. But it ain't precious. Anyone can make a record.

John Lydon •746

We can all make music individually. But we are smart enough to know that the music we make together is far better.

Peter Buck of REM on the band ethic •747

Anybody that forms a group, writes songs and releases records and says they don't care if people like them are complete liars.

James Dean Bradfield of the Manic Street Preachers 2001 •748

Words aren't the salad dressing on the meal of music. Words are the first thing for me. I like having a finished lyric that I'm pleased with, and letting the music follow from there.
Mike Scott of The Waterboys •749

Originally, the function of songs was devotional, I think.
Then in the balladeering centuries, they became a vehicle for the spreading of information, stories and opinions. Now in the 20th century they become a way of making money and achieving fame. I think the other two purposes are much better. Mike Scott of The Waterboys •750

A record doesn't detail a person's changes. If I make a record, that's it. It doesn't affect how I live. And it isn't how I live. It doesn't affect my life, and my life doesn't affect it. What can you say on 40 minutes of wax? Van Morrison 1973 •751

Just because the songs are about reality, there's no reason for music to be boring or depressing. Music is about uplifting people, you know? Shane MacGowan ex-Pogues 1995 •752

It's a great song, it really is. I wish I could remember it.
Shane MacGowan on *Fairytale of New York* •753

The band wanted to know why I wrote miserable songs all the time. I hadn't even noticed.

Natalie Merchant •754

Our music is made from natural impulses. There's no cynical exploitation.

Ed Simons of The Chemical Brothers •755

I'm not a moody songwriter. I don't need to go to the Caribbean to produce. It's a gift from God, it just comes. Smokey Robinson •756

Berry Gordy taught me how to make my songs be a story, with a beginning, a middle, an end and a theme.

Smokey Robinson •757

My songs are my kids and some of them stay with me. Some others I have to send out, out to the war. It might even sound naive, but that's just the way it is.

Thom Yorke of Radiohead 2000 •758

I've always liked a tinge of melancholy in songs, and I find that even on a perfect day anxieties are always close. Tim Finn of Crowded House •759

Going to a 7-eleven in the middle of the night and hearing the clerk whistling one of my songs – that's my idea of a great cover version. Warren Zevon 2000 •760

The verses are the blues, the chorus is the gospel.
Bruce Springsteen 2002 •761

I've always held the song in high regard because songs have got me through so many sinks of dishes and so many humiliating courting events.
Leonard Cohen 1998 •762

Songs do have the power to change things. Music has changed my life, it has changed your life, it has changed everyone's lives. Christy Moore 2006 •763

It's a marvellous feeling when someone says 'I want to do this song of yours' because they've connected to it. That's what I'm after.
Mary Chapin Carpenter •764

You shouldn't have to worry about where you come from. We just want to get good music back on the charts.

Chris Martin of Coldplay 2001 •765

We knew we needed a 'chant' song, because the Bay City Rollers had 'Saturday Night'.

Johnny Ramone discussing the origins of *Blitzkrieg Bop* 2001 •766

The words just came into my head: 'she packed my bags last night, pre-flight. Zero hour is 9 a.m.' I remember jumping out of the car and running into my parents house, shouting, please don't anyone talk to me until I've written this down.

Bernie Taupin on writing *Rocket Man* •767

I don't know why I bother really, because people don't listen to lyrics in rock 'n' roll records too much.

Lou Reed 1989 •768

My vocal style I haven't tried to copy from anyone. It just developed until it became the girlish whine it is today.

Robert Plant •769

I can recall copying the sound of the coalman who used to come round.

Eric Burdon of The Animals •770

If God had nuh given me a song to sing, I wouldn't have a song to sing. The song comes from God, all the time.

Bob Marley •771

Reggae has to be inside you...
Reggae music is simple, all the while...
Cannot be taught, that's a fact.

Bob Marley *Melody Maker*, 1976 •772

I've got a few demons, but I manage to co-exist with 'em. That's what makes you crazy, that's what makes me play my guitar the way I play it sometimes.

Neil Young •773

Heart of Gold put me in the middle of the road. Travelling there soon became a bore so I headed for the ditch. A rougher ride, but I saw more interesting people there.

Neil Young •774

I play the way I do because it allows me to come up with the sickest sounds possible. That's the point now isn't it? Jeff Beck •775

Andy Warhol once said to me, years ago, that I was to music what he was to the visual arts. You can't define it. But it's all happening the way he said it would. The man's amazing. Lou Reed 1974 •776

Lou learned a lot from Andy, mainly about becoming a successful public personality by selling your own private quirks to an audience greedy for more and more geeks.
Lester Bangs on Andy Warhol's influence on Lou Reed (1975) •777

Lou Reed has always epitomised New York for fellow media observers, both in his lifestyle and his art. The chronicler of the shadow world, the deviants, the drug limbo, the concrete jungle, he is the poet laureate of that city. Mick Rock 1972 •778

You're always in the desert looking for an oasis, and all that's out there with you is the piano, this big black beast with 88 teeth. Billy Joel •779

I think Lou writes in a much more detached manner from me. Lou's the kind of guy who sits back and watches what's going on and takes notes... he's a natural journalist. He's almost become a kind of musical Woody Allen...

David Bowie •780

I've still got edge in my music, hopefully always will have – and if my music ever got as laid back as Eric Clapton's I'd pack it in. Or shoot myself. Paul Weller Pass that man a pistol •781

John Fogerty was an Old Testament, shaggy-haired prophet.

Bruce Springsteen on John Fogerty of Creedance Clearwater Revival •782

Some people are very cerebral and can dream a little. We do manual labour.

Jay Farrar of Son Volt, 1995 •783

We took from jazz, old-fashioned rock 'n' roll, the classics. We were musical magpies.

Jon Lord of Deep Purple •784

We just did our own thing: a combination of rock 'n' roll, Fellini, game-show host, corn and mysticism. Fred Schneider B-52's •785

It is an iron law of pop music that if you go away for too long, you come back sounding like the people who've ripped you off in the interim.

Ben Thompson on Television's return in 1992 •786

Waits is an originator without being the least bit original. He was the first in a long line of white spade urban rock 'n' roll poets who chose to romanticise the sleazy side of the tracks. This approach had been done to death in the literature of the Beat Generation, but Waits was the first to successfully bring it above ground on vinyl.

Terri A. Huggins •787

I'm what they used to call a troubadour. What I do for a living is to get people to feeling good. Willie Nelson •788

The best country music is incredibly simple, yet very poignant and moving.

Emmylou Harris •789

You've got to have smelled a lot of mule manure before you can sing like a hillbilly.
Hank Williams quoted by Tony Palmer in 1976 •790

I don't like country music – but don't mean to denigrate those who do. For those people who like country music, denigrate means to put down. Bob Newhart •791

If you are a songwriter, did anyone ask you if you wanted to spend the rest of your career modifying your lyric content to suit the spiritual needs of an imaginary eleven-year-old?

Frank Zappa *The Real Frank Zappa Book* 1989 •792

For a start, I've got to be out of my head to write.

Shane MacGowan of The Pogues 1989 •793

It's easier to write about things that are falling apart than things that are beautiful and perfect. Beck 1996 •794

It's actually really hard to write a happy song without sounding corny.

Carl Bell of Fuel 2001 •795

Listen, the easiest way to get laid by a girl, or get rid of her, is to write a song about her. David Crosby
1970's •796

I try to bring back some intelligence to music,
instead of just four chords and dumb lyrics.
I'll match the power of my ballads with anything
Nirvana are doing. Barry Manilow Hmmm •797

The trick of writing is to make it sound like it's all happening for the first time.
Tim Buckley •798

People think it's glamorous, songwriting, but
this is what it's really about, walking around
singing to yourself like a loony. Elvis Costello
1995 •799

We're the best of friends, but always fighting. It was there right from the beginning. There has to be creative tension.
Stewart Copeland of Police, 1985 •800

It's a physical, emotional, and intellectual process. Not to sound too high falutin' about it, but it's an immediate process that involves all my faculties. It's an interplay between the conscious and subconscious. Moby 2000 •801

Pete, as far as writing songs goes and coming up with general basic ideas, he's fantastic. But Pete Townshend is not The Who. And I think the first person to admit that will be Pete Townshend. And you've got to realise that. The Who is four people. Roger Daltrey 1976 •802

I write a song because I am deeply moved to write a song. It's a very simple process in that way.
Adam Duritz of Counting Crows 1996 •803

To me, songwriting is almost like stamp collecting – except that I collect fragments of other peoples lives.

David Gedge of The Wedding Present 1993 •804

I tried to write these meaningful songs and always, the whole time, I would come back to monkeys and chickens and frogs. Chris Balew of The Presidents of The United States 1995 •805

When I'm writing my songs, I get to parts of me I've hidden for so long. And it's a liberating place to be.
Tori Amos 1996 •806

I write for myself and I try to make it something I would listen to. I operate under the idea that I'm not unusual. And if I try to do it really well for myself, other people can relate to it, too. But I don't really know how to write for other people so I can't do that. Lou Reed 1998 •807

I've written most of my best songs driving on a long journey scribbling lyrics on cigarette packets whilst steering. Neil Young •808

Those first five or six songs that I wrote, I was just taking notes at a fantastic rock concert that was going on inside my head. And once I had written the songs, I had to sing them.

Jim Morrison •809

I always make sure I have a guitar around. I might suddenly get an idea for a song. I don't sit around saying: now I'm going to write a song. they come to me. I firmly believe they're floating through the room right now. You don't create them, you find them.

Keith Richards •810

Whenever I don't know what to write about, I just close my eyes and think of Essex.

Damon Albarn in *Blah Blah Blah* magazine, 1996 •811

I don't think songwriters listen to themselves talk. They fall into rock cliches. That's what I try to avoid.

Aimee Mann •812

I've never been interested in writing pop songs. I don't consider myself part of pop music at all. Lou Reed •813

I write pop songs. But I think it is sprinkled with a lot of counter-culture references. It ranged from rap to hip hop to trip hop, house, drum and bass, and experimental and improv and jazz. Nelly Furtado •814

I guess I just lucked out that I like writing songs and people like my songs. That's the catch. You do what you like and that's fine, but if no one else likes it, eventually, you run out of steam.

Wayne Coyne of The Flaming Lips 1999 •815

When you stop putting yourself on the line, and you don't touch your own heart, how do you expect to touch other people?

Tori Amos •816

19

I want to be Bob Dylan
Mr Jones wishes he was someone just a little more funky.
When everybody loves you, son that's just about as funky as you can be.
`Counting Crows` *Mr Jones* (words: Adam Duritz) (1994) from the album *August and Everything After* •817

MR JONES

The songs are insanely honest, not meanin' to twist any head, and written only for the reason that I myself, me alone wanted and needed to write them. `Bob Dylan` 1964 •819

Fame threw me for a loop at first. I learned how to swim with it and turned it around. So you can just throw it in the closet and pick it up when you need it. `Bob Dylan` •818

In writing songs I've learned as much from Cezanne as I have from Woody Guthrie.

`Bob Dylan` quoted in *Behind The Shades,* by Clinton Heylin, 1991 •820

The folk music scene had been like a paradise that I had to leave, like Adam had to leave the garden. It was just too perfect. Bob Dylan *Chronicles* •821

An easy way out would be to say, 'yes, it's all behind me, that's it and there's no more.' But you want to say that there might be a small chance that something up there will surpass whatever you did. Everybody works in the shadow of what they've previously done. But you have to overcome that. Bob Dylan 1989 •822

I went over my whole life. I went over my whole childhood. I didn't talk to anyone for a week after Elvis died. If it wasn't for Elvis and Hank Williams, I wouldn't be doing what I do today. Bob Dylan 1978 •823

There was a presence in the room that couldn't have been anybody but Jesus. I truly had a born-again experience, if you want to call it that. Jesus put his hand on me. It was a physical thing. I felt it. I felt it all over me. I felt my whole body tremble. The glory of the Lord knocked me down and picked me up. Bob Dylan on his experience in a Tuscon hotel room, November 1978 •824

The closest I ever got to the sound I hear in my mind was on individual bands in the Blonde on Blonde album. It's that thin, that wild mercury sound. It's metallic and bright gold, with whatever that conjures up. That's my particular sound. Bob Dylan 1978 •825

I knew that when I got into folk music it was more of a serious type thing. The songs were filled with more despair, more sadness, more triumph, more faith in the supernatural, much deeper feelings... life is full of complexities, and rock and roll didn't reflect that. Bob Dylan •826

Mr Hammond asked me if I wanted to sing any of them over again and I said no. I can't see myself singing the same song twice in a row. That's terrible. Bob Dylan on recording his debut album in 1961 •827

I was completely taken over by him. He was like a guide.
Bob Dylan on Woody Guthrie •828

What's money? A man is a success if he gets up in the morning and gets to bed at night and in between he does what he wants to. Bob Dylan •829

I like those people who come to see me now. They're not aware of my early days, but I'm glad of that. It lifts that burden of responsibility, of having to play everything exactly like it was on some certain record. I can't do that. Which way the wind is blowing, they're going to come out different every time. Bob Dylan 1998 •830

MR JONES

If I had a good quote, I'd be wearing it.

Bob Dylan in reply to a French journalist who asked for 'a good quote', quoted in *The Times,* July 1981 •831

I think that's just another word for a washed-up has-been.

Bob Dylan on being an 'Icon' •832

Actually, I never liked Dylan's kind of music before, I always thought he sounded like Yogi Bear.

Mick Ronson •833

I did Dylan, and he fucked me over. I hate that guy. That was the most miserable session, too. I did a really good job on it, and he kept my playing on there even when the advance copies went to the record company. Then at the last moment he took it off because he said it sounded too much like Guns n' Roses. Why did he call me, y'know?

Slash 1991 •834

This voice was like broken glass, like spitting. The words were like arrows, being shot straight into the heart of the establishment. That was what made me realise what the words of a song could do.

Bernie Taupin on hearing *The Times They Are A Changin',* 1964 •835

Dylan was, like many young people who admired him, a disturbed, unconventional, rebellious and confused internal exile from affluence he could have had, but did not want.

Lawrence Goldman *Studies on the Left,* 1968 •836

He was rarely tender, and seldom reached out to anticipate another's needs, though occasionally he would exhibit a sudden concern for another outlaw, hitchhiker, or bung, and got out of his way to see them looked after.

Joan Baez 1988 •837

I had never been on a professional, big-time session with studio musicians. I didn't know anything. I liked the songs. If you'd been there, you would have seen it was a very disorganised, weird scene. Since then I've played on millions of sessions and I realise how really weird that Dylan session was.

Mike Bloomfield 1968 •838

The Chimes of Freedom shows that his love of the majestic, big, epic type of material is all but a permanent side of Bob Dylan. How many artists would come right out and say they are singing for 'every hung-up person in the whole wide universe'? John Landau in *Crawdaddy* •839

By today's standards it wasn't very loud, but by those standards of the day was the loudest thing anybody had ever heard... there were arguments between people sitting next to each other. Some people were booing, some people were cheering.

Joe Boyd on Dylan's famous first electric performance at Newport •840

Highway 61 re-invented rock 'n' roll in a way perhaps only half a dozen albums have done in the 40 year history of the art.

Clinton Heylin in *Behind The Shades* 1991 •841

Dylan was 25. In just five years he had transformed popular music beyond recognition, making rock 'n' roll capable of saying a great deal more than just Awopbopaloobop, and had been vilified, glorified, even deified for his trouble.

Clinton Heylin in *Behind The Shades* 1991 •842

Bob's music really is dependent on catching the moment – they're like snapshots, Polaroids. The first take is gonna be better even if it's got some wrong notes.

Rob Stoner Dylan's bass player on the *Desire* album •843

The nature of the artist is that he keeps going. The paradox of the audience is that we love him for this, and yet we want him to stop and stay in the place where he touched us last, or most.

Paul Williams in *Bob Dylan, Performing Artist* 1990 •844

Dylan to me is the perfect symbol of the anti-artist in our society. He is against everything – the last resort of someone who doesn't really want to change the world... Dylan's songs accept the world as it is.

Ewan MacColl on Bob Dylan, *Melody Maker*, 1965 •845

Bob Dylan's music is the greatest music ever written, to me. The man says it all, exactly the right way. Incredibly powerful. You don't get no more intense.

Bruce Springsteen 1980 •846

Watching this programme, there are moments when you'd swear that Bob Dylan was actually dead, in so emphatically past tense is the story told, so respectful, indeed quietly monumental is its tone. The voice-over could almost be reciting his obituary from *The Times.*

And then, almost at the last minute in the final section which telescopes the last two decades into a fifth of the running time, the mood suddenly switches and we are reassured that Bob, far from being busy dyin', is busy being reborn (and not for the first time). Mat Snow on *Bob Dylan: The American Troubadour,* for *Rock's Backpages,* March 2001 •847

She don't like slavery
She won't sit and beg
Billy Idol *Rebel Yell* (1984)
from the album *Rebel Yell* •848

REBEL

If there's a problem, you have to go out and solve it.

Bob Geldof •849

No, Prime Minister, nothing is as simple as dying.

Bob Geldof remonstrates with Margaret Thatcher •850

People are dying NOW.
Give us the money NOW.
Give me the money now.

Geldof at Live Aid •851

Fuck the address, just give the phone, here's the number...

Geldof at Live Aid, oft misquoted as 'give us yer fucking money...' •852

I've just realized that today is the best day of my life. Now I'm going home to sleep.

Geldof at Live Aid •853

Not to be immodest, but the first one was perfect in almost every sense... Artistically, people seemed to up the ante, and the performances were pretty great across the board. Huge amounts of money were raised, not a penny lost, and politically it elevated the issue onto the global table. The whole thing just worked, unbelievably. Geldof at Live Aid •854

One can have great concern for the people of Ethiopia, but it's another thing to inflict daily torture on the people of England. Morrissey on the Band Aid song •855

Edge can say more about the struggle in El Salvador with his guitar than the written word.
Bono •856

This musical thing been here since America been here. This is trial and tribulation music.
Mahalia Jackson gospel singer and civil rights activist, in *Time* magazine, 1968 •857

Until the philosophy which holds one race superior and one inferior is finally and permanently discredited and abandoned, everywhere is war. Bob Marley *War,* 1976 •858

God never made no difference between black, white, blue, pink or green. People is people, y'know.
Bob Marley •859

Here was this Third World superstar emerging, an individual against the system with an incredible look: this was the first time you had seen anyone looking like that, other than Jimi Hendrix. And Bob had that power about him and incredible lyrics.

Chris Blackwell on Bob Marley •860

You can blow out a candle
But you can't blow out a fire
Once the flames begin to catch
The wind will blow it higher.

Peter Gabriel *Biko,* (1980) from
the third *Peter Gabriel* album •861

Tyler is guilty, the white judge has said so,
What right do we have to say it's not so?

UB40 *Tyler,* (1980) from the album *Signing Off* •862

You caught me on the loose, fighting to be free
Now you show me a noose on the cotton tree.
Entertainment for you, martyrdom for me.

Third World *96° In The Shade,* (1977) from
the album *96° In The Shade* •863

Jesus said, I believe it's true
The red folk are in the sunset too.
Stole their land, they won't give it back
And they sent Geronimo a Cadillac.

Dick Gaughan *Geronimo's Cadillac,* (1996)
from the album *Sail On* •864

We're tired of beating our head against the wall
And working for someone else.
We're people, we're like the birds and the bees
But we'd rather die on our feet than keep living on our knees.

James Brown *Say It Loud, I'm Black and I'm Proud,*
(with Alfred Ellis) (1969) •865

They have the authority to kill a minority.
Fuck that shit, cause I ain't the one,
For a punk mother fucker with a badge and a gun,
To be beatin' on, and throw in jail. N.W.A. *Fuck Tha Police,* (1989) from
the album *Straight Outta Compton* •866

Justice costs. It's for people who can really afford justice. So music fills the place of working man's justice.

Ben Harper •867

Get up, stand up
Stand up for your rights. Get up, stand up
Don't give up the fight.

Bob Marley & The Wailers *Get Up, Stand Up* (1973)
from the album *Burnin'* •868

A working class hero is something to be
If you want to be a hero then just follow me.

John Lennon *Working Class Hero* (1970)
from the album *John Lennon and The Plastic Ono Band* •869

We're not preachers, and we're not leaders. Our fans see us as people who are saying exactly what they'd like to say in our position.
Simon Friend of The Levellers •870

You've got to walk it like you talk it, or else you're just exploiting it, don't you think? It's hard to find a way to do that.
Billy Bragg •871

I don't think people are converted to socialism by eye contact with me. Billy Bragg 1997 •872

Ev'rywhere I hear the sound of marching, charging feet, boy, 'Cause the summer's here and the time is right for fighting in the street, boy'.
Rolling Stones *Street Fighting Man* (Jagger & Richards) (1968) from the album *Beggars Banquet* •873

They say sing while you slave and I just get bored. I ain't gonna work on Maggie's farm no more.
Bob Dylan *Maggie's Farm* (1965) from the album Bringing It All Back Home •874

A septic isle – grey, boring, shitty. The inner city kids weren't alright.
Ian Dury on 70s Britain •875

It's just a rumour that was spread around town,
Somebody said that someone got filled in
For saying that people get killed in
The result of this shipbuilding.

Elvis Costello *Shipbuilding* (1983) a song inspired by
the Falkland's War; from the album *Punch the Clock* •876

> When they kick at your front door
> How you gonna come?
> With your hands on your head,
> Or on the trigger of your gun?
>
> The Clash *The Guns of Brixton* (Simenon) (1979)
> from the album *London Calling* •877

> Nat-West Barclays Midlands Lloyds
> Blackhorse Apocalypse
> Death sanitised through credit.
>
> Manic Street Preachers
> *Natwest-Barclays-Midlands-Lloyds* (words: Wire / James)
> (1992) from the album *Generation Terrorists* •878

> They smelt of pubs, and Wormwood scrubs
> And too many right-wing meetings.
> The Jam *Down In The Tube Station At Midnight*
> (Weller) (1978) from the album *All Mod Cons* •879

Now it seems to me to be such a cruel irony
He's richer now than he ever was before.
Now my cheque is all spent, and I can't afford the rent
There's one law for the rich, one for the poor.

Christy Moore *Ordinary Man* (1985) from the album *Ordinary Man* •880

> What chance have you got 'gainst a tie and a crest?
> The Jam *Eton Rifles* (Weller) (1979) *Setting Sons* •881

Out the club about three, to the take-away,
The shit-in-a-tray merchants, shops got special perchant for the disorderly.
Geezerz looking ordinary and a few looking leary,
Chips fly round the sound of the latest chart entry,
An incendiary waiting to blast.

Street *Geezers Need Excitement* (2002) from the
album *Original Pirate Material* •882

I believe everything we dream
Can come to pass through our union.
We can turn the world around,
We can turn the earth's revolution.
We have the power.

Patti Smith *People Have The Power* (1988)
from the album *Dream Of Life* •883

As long as I'm attacked by the KGB and the CIA, then I'm probably on the right track. Joan Baez 1988 •884

At the end of every hard-earned day
People find some reason to believe.

Bruce Springsteen *Reason To Believe* (1982)
from the album *Nebraska* •885

Daddy worked his whole life, for nothing but the pain,
Now he walks these empty rooms looking for something to blame.
You inherit the sins, you inherit the flames,
Adam raised a Cain.

Bruce Springsteen *Adam Raised A Cain* (1978) from
the album *Darkness OnThe Edge Of Town* •886

How does it feel
To be without a home
Like a complete unknown
Like a rolling stone?

Bob Dylan *Like A Rolling Stone* (1965)
from the album *Highway 61 Revisted* •887

I'm interested in anything about revolt, disorder, chaos, especially activity that appears to have no meaning. It seems to me to be the road toward freedom.

Jim Morrison *Time* magazine, 1968 •888

You know you can't hold me forever,
I didn't sign up with you.
I'm not a present for your friends to open,
This boy's too young to be singing the blues.

Elton John *Goodbye Yellow Brick Road* (words: Bernie Taupin), (1973)
from the album *Goodbye Yellow Brick Road* •889

I'm tired of the excuses everybody uses,
He's your kid – do as you see fit.
But get this through that I don't approve
Of what you did to your own flesh and blood.

10,000 Maniacs *What's The Matter Here?*
(words: Natalie Merchant) (1987) from the album
In My Tribe •890

If I'm more of an influence to your son as a rapper than you are as a father... you got to look at yourself as a parent.

Ice Cube *Rolling Stone,* 1994 •891

Tolling for the aching ones whose wounds cannot be nursed,
For the countless confused, accused, misused, strung-out ones an' worse.
An' for every hung-up person in the whole wide universe.
An' we gazed upon the chimes of freedom flashing.
Bob Dylan *Chimes of Freedom* (1964) from the album
Another Side Of Bob Dylan •892

I still don't know who the fuck I am. I know what I don't believe in. I know what I've rejected. But I don't know what I do believe in. Trent Reznor of Nine Inch Nails (1995) •893

Freedom's just another word for nothing left to lose.
Kris Kristofferson *Me and Bobby McGhee* (1969) •894

As a revolutionary and leader of people at the barricades, I failed. But as a person who inwardly revolts all the time, I'm a raging success.

Roy Harper •895

If you don't confront censorship, then the music of confrontational artists will be silenced.

Tom Morello of Rage Against The Machine, 1993 •896

When you get your ass kicked that hard, it makes you go to the innermost depths of what you are all about as a human being. Now, maybe most people have not been kicked that hard, but it's still in everybody, and this music rings a bell that you can hear throughout the fucking world. Quincy Jones talking about the blues.
Rolling Stone, 1976 •897

We always set out to make records about ideas and attitudes that are important and real: the band we never had when we were growing up.

Richie Edwards of Manic Street Preachers •898

We never thought of it as being any great statement – it was just the way Black Flag did things.

Greg Ginn •899

I never tackled an issue, social, political or otherwise, unless there was a metaphor in which to dress it up. I was never into writing propaganda or polemic.

Sting 2000 •900

If ever I would stop thinking about music and politics
I would tell you that music is the expression of emotion
and that politics is merely the decoy of perception.

The Disposable Heroes of Hiphoprisy
Music and Politics (1992) from the album
Hypocrisy Is the Greatest Luxury •901

I want to do anything I can to promote AIDS education,
awareness, prevention – whatever. I think because I'm
a celebrity, a public person, I have a real responsibility
to be a spokesperson. Next to Hitler, AIDS is the worst
thing to happen to the 20th century. Madonna •902

I have this kinda naive idea that the world should be a
different place than it is right now, and I'd like to be
involved in changing it by trying to understand more
and be honest about my understanding.

Moby 1999 •903

As much as I love making records, I do feel a certain
amount of guilt, firstly, being part of a consumer society,
and, second, generating all this plastic and bleached
paper. I figure if I'm going to make CDs, I might as well
try and communicate something that at least I think is
important, for, to, people. Moby 2001 •904

There's no point in being subversive in rock anymore,
there's no way you can be – unless you ram a stick of
dynamite up your ass. Kurt Cobain of Nirvana 1992 •905

I want someone to rob a bank in the name of Green Day. I want them to make masks of our faces and rob a fucking bank.

Billie Joe Armstrong of Green Day 1997 •906

If this was a slightly more primitive time
I would already be burning at the stake.
I expect there is still time for that.

Morrissey 1989 •907

I am an anti-Christ
I am an anarchist
Don't know what I want but I know where to get it
I wanna destroy passers-by
Because I wanna be anarchy.

Sex Pistols *Anarchy In The UK* (1976) from the album *Never Mind The Bollocks...* •908

You say you want a revolution
Well you know
We all want to change the world.

The Beatles *Revolution* (Lennon & McCartney) (1968) from *The Beatles* (The White Album) •909

Imagine there's no heaven
It's easy if you try.
No hell below us,
Above us, only sky.
Imagine all the people,
Living for today.

John Lennon *Imagine* (1971) from the album *Imagine* •910

These days, everyone wants John Lennon's sunglasses, accent and swagger, but no one is prepared to take their clothes off and stand naked like he did in his songs. Putting your head over the parapet means something completely different these days, but it's still a big part of what rock and roll is all about for me. You have to use your celebrity, negotiate your position and be aware that celebrity can diminish a cause as much as illuminate it. **Bono** 2000 •911

Neil Tennant: As if people think, 'oh, we think war's fantastic, actually, but I've now changed my mind because John Lennon's told me peace is a good thing.'
Chris Lowe: He's enough to make you want to go to war, John Lennon.

The Pet Shop Boys on Lennon's legacy •912

War!
What is it good for?
Absolutely nothing.

Edwin Starr *War*
(Norman Whitfield & Barrett Strong)
(1970) from the album *War And Peace* •913

Body bags and dropping bombs
The pentagon knows how to turn us on

L7 *Wargasm* (1992) from the album *Bricks Are Heavy* •914

Democracy don't rule the world,
You'd better get that in your head.
This world is ruled by violence,
But I guess that's better left unsaid.

Bob Dylan *Union Sundown* (1983)
from the album *Infidels* •915

In our lifetime those who kill,
The newsworld hands them stardom.

Morrissey *The Last of the Famous International Playboys* (1989)
from the album *Viva Hate* •916

I'm for nuclear power, but I haven't told
anyone because I am still hoping to fuck
Jane Fonda like everybody dreams of doing
who's involved in the No Nuke movement.

Pete Townshend •917

Everything went downhill from the moment McDonald's
was given a license to invade England... To me, it was
like the outbreak of war and I couldn't understand why
English troops weren't retaliating. Morrissey *The Guardian,*
1994 •918

Hey, farmer farmer, put away that DDT now
Give me spots on my apples, but leave me the birds and the bees, please.

Joni Mitchell *Big Yellow Taxi* (1970)
from the album *Ladies Of The Canyon* •919

As rock stars we witnessed the flowering of
a new consciousness founded on sex, drugs,
rock and the renunciation of Americana.

John Phillips of the Mamas and Papas •920

On (the day of the attack) the victims were American. But the horrible scenes that we're witnessed on TV this week are regular occurrences in other places around the globe. And too often, violence like this has been meted out by our own country and its client states. We should stand together against this type of violence in all its forms, whenever it happens, whether it is done in the name of religious fanaticism, or in the name of our own domestic elite.

Tom Morello of Rage Against The Machine, on 9/11 •921

I don't like you. I don't like your boss. I don't like what you did. Thank you.

Bruce Springsteen declines an audience with Oliver North, offered via North's secretary in 1988 •922

Down in the shadow of the penitentiary
Out by the gas fires of the refinery.
I'm ten years burning down the road,
Nowhere to run ain't got nowhere to go.

Bruce Springsteen Born In The USA (1984)
from the album Born In The USA •923

The guy in 'Born In The USA' wants to strip away that mythic America which was Reagan's image of America. He wants to find something real and connecting. He's looking for a home in his country. Bruce Springsteen 1987 •924

**I wouldn't say a single word to them, I would listen
to what they have to say and that's what no one did.**

Marilyn Manson when asked what he would say to the kids in Columbine,
where a massacre was enacted and people pointed the finger at his influence •925

**Anybody intelligent enough to realize what America is,
is not going to sit around and do nothing about it.
They're going to be the same way that I am. They're
going to be the same way our fans are.
They're going to be pissed.**

Marilyn Manson •926

**I was waiting for some young singer to come along,
to write these songs and stand up. I waited a long time.**

Neil Young is, not unreasonably, disappointed with the younger generation's
failure to register their disapproval of the Bush regime •927

**Don't want to be an American idiot
Don't want a nation under the new mania.
Can you hear the sound of hysteria?
The subliminal mind-fuck America.**

Green Day American Idiot (2004)
from the album American Idiot •928

All the great political music was made
at the height of political confrontations

Billy Bragg •929

You can't trust politicians. It doesn't matter
who makes a political speech. It's all lies...
and it applies to any rock star who wants
to make a political speech as well.

Bob Geldof •930

And Pontiff, pretty Pontiff,
Can anyone shake your hand?
Or is just that you like uniforms
And someone kissing your hand?

Lou Reed *Good Evening Mr Waldheim* (1989)
from the album *New York* •931

Walking through the doors at 10 Downing Street,
not as a plumber, but an invited guest. I'm glad
I did it to have a look, but in terms of New Labour,
I recognise now that we were conned. We thought
Tony Blair was John F. Kennedy, when in fact he
was John Major with a better PR team.

Noel Gallagher 2001 •932

Every time I come back to Britain from elsewhere
I get pissed off. It's the civil liberties thing.
Even when people are partying on the Berlin
Wall, you can't do it near the M25.

Will of The Shamen, 1990 •933

When you realize that all governments fail at one time or another, it takes the shine off of democracy and all of its speeches and policies. You realize it's all an empty she-bang.

Joe Strummer 2001 •934

Most governments don't last as long as this band.

Peter Buck of R.E.M. 1998 •935

Left wing, chicken wing, it don't make no difference to me.

Woody Guthrie •936

The lame part of the Sixties was the political part, the social part. The real part was the spiritual part.

Jerry Garcia •937

Every rebellion is co-opted and in 50 years is seen as a natural progression from what came before.

Stephen Malkmus of Pavement, 1994 •938

Messages become a drag like preaching. I think one of the worst possible beliefs is that pop stars know more about life than anyone else.

Nick Mason of Pink Floyd •939

PLANET CLAIRE

Planet Claire has pink air
All the trees are red.
No one ever dies there
No one has a head.

B52's *Planet Claire* •940

FROM THE INDULGENT...

If you looked up the word 'pretentious' in the dictionary, you could possibly see a picture of Emerson, Lake and Palmer.

`Carl Palmer` •941

Copeland heard my arrangement of Hoe-down and he was knocked out by it... We'd altered it with a very finely dotted quaver because it didn't swing the other way. `Keith Emerson` •942

It's not art in the same way as painting a picture.

`Keith Emerson` Oh really, Keith? How f***ing enlightening •943

Jazz is an ocean. Rock 'n' roll is a swimming pool. I hang out on a lake.

`Carlos Santana` •944

If art were to redeem man, it could do so only by saving him from the seriousness of life, and restoring him to an unexpected boyishness.

`John Lennon` •945

People described her voice as everything from eerie to bland and smooth, to wind in a drainpipe, to an IBM computer with a Garbo accent.

Andy Warhol on Nico •946

Yes and Genesis are as exciting as a used Kleenex.

Nick Lowe •947

Like a foul alignment of all the black planets, this collection of 95-97 material culled from the Keys to Ascension I and II albums, saw all the important members of Yes [...] reunited to wreak havoc on the world. Chords are played at random, tunes change tempo for no other reason than that is what happens in symphonies and tracks are long just for longness's sake... The fact that they had a hit single as recently as 15 years ago should serve as a warning to us all that this sort of thing could strike at any moment. David Quantick reviews Yes's album *Keys to the Studio* in *Q Magazine*, September 2001 •948

Our music has depth, and attempts philosophical thought and meaning with discussions of infinity, eternity and mortality. There is a line which people cross that turns it into some magical, mystical realm, for which I don't claim responsibility and don't hold any great truck with.

Dave Gilmour of Pink Floyd •949

Above all, Roxy Music is a state of mind. Hollywood movies meets English art school, with a little Schopenhauer thrown in, both in the lyrics I write and the way we look. Of course, that allows for all kinds of possibilities. I am, you might say, a collagiste.
Bryan Ferry 1975. Actually we prefer pretentious w***er, Bryan •950

He wanted to combine the fastidiousness of art with the sweat of rock 'n' roll music. He explains this in a set speech, then apologises for having delivered it. Philip Norman
on Bryan Ferry •951

Ambient Music must be able to accommodate many levels of listening attention without enforcing one in particular; it must be as ignorable as it is interesting.
Brian Eno sleevenotes to *Music For Airports*, 1979 •952

Analysis is like a lobotomy. Who wants to have all their edges shaved off? David Byrne •953

To sing is to love and to affirm, to fly and soar, to coast into the hearts of the people who listen, to tell them that life is to live, that love is there, that nothing is a promise, but that beauty exists, and must be hunted for and found. Joan Baez *Daybreak*, 'Singing', 1970 •954

Please don't write that we eat.
We don't want the fans to think that we eat.

Robin Guthrie of The Cocteau Twins •955

The greatest conflicts
are not between two
people but between one
person and himself.

Garth Brooks How profound. •956

Am I a fruitcake? I don't
know. Perception is reality.
What you see me as in
your world is what I am; it
doesn't matter what I am.

Macy Gray •957

If music be the food of love
Then laughter is its Queen.
And likewise if behind is in front,
Then dirt in truth is clean.

Procol Harum *A Whiter Shade of Pale,* (1967)
from the album *Procol Harum* •958

I like our name because its so easy to spell.
It's real authentic. It's pop art, in a sense.

Ric Ocasek of The Cars •959

Supernature is a story of good and evil.
What I want to say to people is to leave
each thing in its proper place, otherwise
the monsters will be coming. Cerrone •960

I hope to refine music, study it, try to find some area that I can unlock. I don't quite know how to explain it but it's there. These can't be the only notes in the world, there's got to be other notes some place, in some dimension, between the cracks on the piano keys.

Marvin Gaye •961

We come from the land of the ice and snow,
From the midnight sun where the hot springs blow.
The hammer of the gods will drive our ships to new lands,
To fight the horde, singing and crying: Valhalla, I am coming!

Led Zeppelin *The Immigrant Song,* (1970) from the album *Led Zeppelin III* •962

My records are built like a Wagnerian opera; they start simply and they end with dynamic force, meaning and purpose. Phil Spector •963

We play the machines, but the machines also play us.

Ralf Hutter of Kraftwerk •964

Just 'cause you feel it doesn't mean it's there.

Radiohead *There There,* (2003), from the album *Hail To The Thief* •965

**Music has ceased to belong to the young...
the rock rebel is defunct. He's meaningless.**

Sting *Smash Hits,* 1982 •966

I think quotes are very
dangerous things. Kate Bush •967

I had a shrink when I was in the nuthouse,
and he gave me one good rule that's stuck
with me. He said, 'Before you do anything,
ask yourself; am I going to get away with it?'

Iggy Pop •968

**I'm not a tortured artist,
and there's nothing really
wrong with me. I just had
a bad time for a while.**

Elliott Smith 2001 •969

THROUGH THE DELUSIONAL...

God made me – but I created the myth. James Brown •970

I've outdone anyone you can name – Mozart, Beethoven, Bach, Strauss. Irving Berlin, he wrote 1,001 tunes. I wrote 5,500. James Brown •971

I think I'm right on the threshold of bursting through. I feel I'm as good as Beethoven or any of the greats. I don't compare myself to Beethoven, I must make that clear. I just think that I'm capable of all that he was capable of. Marvin Gaye 1973 •972

I'm an artist and that means I can be as egotistical as I want to be.
Lou Reed 1998 •973

My style of music is so far out in its own field that I don't even want to explain it. It's gone beyond the point where I can communicate it on a verbal level.

Iggy Pop 1972 •974

How can you consider flower power outdated?
The essence of my lyrics is the desire for peace
and harmony. That's all anyone has ever wanted.
How could it become outdated? Robert Plant •975

Salvador Dali showed me
that everything was possible.

Edgar Froese of Tangerine Dream •976

I could sing like Caruso if I wanted to,
but he's already done it. Tom Waits •977

My art is more important to me than just
being remembered as the person who got
five million to be sponsored by Coca-Cola.
Terence Trent D'Arby •978

I happen to believe I'm a genius. As time proves
me right, I'm becoming less and less afraid to say so.
Terence Trent D'Arby 1988 •979

Art is born inside someone and comes out into something
that you can experience and that's all it is. There's no
difference between Beethoven and Johnny Rotten.
There's no difference between Beethoven and me.
Adam Duritz of Counting Crows, 1998. Yes there is. •980

I believe our purpose is to inspire and guide the human race.

Sinead O'Connor on the nature of pop music, *The Independent,* 1991 •981

I could not take the brunt of standing in the light of my own work. There was a Faustian bargain I could not make. I could have you mock me for wearing funny clothes, that I could deal with. But I couldn't deal with actually standing in the light of my own musical power. Billy Corgan •982

I think we're relevant, we're important! We're exciting, mind expanding!

Ian Brown of The Stone Roses •983

We're the most important group in the world, because we've got the best songs and we haven't even begun to show our potential yet.

Ian Brown 1990 •984

Anybody's first two albums against my first two albums, I'm there. I'm with The Beatles.

Noel Gallagher 1996. No you're not •985

I would hope we mean more to people than putting money in a church basket and saying ten Hail Marys on a Sunday. Has God played Knebworth recently?

Noel Gallagher *NME*, 1997 •986

...TO THE DOWNRIGHT BONKERS

I feel safe in white because, deep down inside, I'm an angel.

Puff Daddy •987

I don't exist. Tap my head and it sounds like metal. I walk across the sun and I don't cast a shadow.

Brett Anderson of Suede, 1994 •988

Gibby Haynes of Butthole Surfers •989

I don't go looking for weird shit, but it seems like it comes for me.

A lot of people think I'm clinically mad.

Morrissey 1986 •990

I'm naive in a Luke Skywalker way. Not intuitive or smart enough to be a Darth Vader. Ryan Adams of Whiskeytown, 2001 •991

If I want a sound, I usually feel better if I've chased it and killed it, skinned it and cooked it.

Tom Waits •992

It was only four tracks written on the machine, but I was picking up twenty from the extra-terrestrial squad. I am the dub shepherd. Lee 'Scratch' Perry •993

He was a freak and I was a freak, so we decided to freak together.

Flea on Chili's bandmate Anthony Kiedis •994

I've got a very irregular head.

Syd Barrett 1971 •995

In a cybernetic fit of rage
She pissed off to another age
She lives in 1999
With her new boyfriend, a blob of slime.
Each time I see a translucent face
I remember the monster from outer space.

John Cooper Clarke *i married a monster from outer space,* (1978) from the album *Disguise In Love* •996

I'm gonna give up playing piano. I'm gonna become a rock and roll suicide, take my nasty out and piddle all over the front row, just to get rid of my staid old image. Elton John 1974 •997

I'm gonna put on an iron shirt
And chase Satan outta church.

Max Romeo *Chase The Devil* (Max Romeo, Lee Perry) (1976) •998

I wish people would turn off their computers, go outside, talk to people, touch people, lick people, enjoy each other's company and smell each other on the rump. Tre Cool •999

It's on Amerika's tortured brow
That Mickey Mouse has grown up a cow.
Now the workers have struck for fame,
'Cause Lennon's on sale again.

David Bowie *Life On Mars?* (1973)
from the album *Hunky Dory* •1000

I like my pussy. Sometimes I stare at it in the mirror when I'm undressing and wonder what it would look like without any hair like when I was a baby. Sometimes I sit at the edge of the bed and spred my legs. And stare into the mirror and wonder what others see. Sometimes I stick my finger in my pussy and wiggle it around the dark wetness and feel what a cock or a tongue must feel when I'm sitting on it. I pull my finger out and I always taste and smell it. It's hard to describe, it smells like a baby to me, fresh and full of life. Madonna in her
Sex book •1001

I'm just SO abstract. I'm so Jackson Pollock! Talking a load of old Pollocks.
Beth Orton •1002

The premise behind Oingo Boingo is to remain in a state of motion, bouncing – boinging along, if you will – and to try to present something that is fun and entertaining but also has a point of view.
Danny Elfman with his band's mission statement •1003

Gwar was created by the master of creation, an ambiguous being named Larry, as the ultimate doomsday device.
Oderous Urungus delivers another mission statement •1004

I'm the artist formerly known as Beck. I have a genius wig.
When I put that wig on, then the true genius emerges. I don't have enough hair to be a genius. I think you have to have hair going everywhere.
Beck •1005

We all had our childhoods, and we all know how important the balloon was.

Nena she of 99 of them, all red •1006

I love *ET* 'cos it reminds me of me. This person is like 800 years old and he's filling you with all kinds of wisdom.

Michael Jackson •1007

They're about to poke their genitals into our cream cheese moon right now. That's my eye; the moon is part of me. Why don't they poke it in the sun? They're not very daring.

Captain Beefheart's take on the moon landing in 1969 •1008

**You're like my yo-yo that glowed in the dark
What made it special made it dangerous
So I bury it and forget.**

Kate Bush *Cloudbusting* (1985) from the album *Hounds Of Love* •1009

When I'm no longer rapping, I want to open up an ice cream parlour and call myself Scoop Dogg.

Snoop Dogg •1010

I like to go to the graveyard, lay down on somebody's grave, take a bottle out there, dance around naked, y'know?

Tom Waits 1983 •1011

There are only forty people in the world, and five of them are hamburgers.

Captain Beefheart •1012

I have a clairvoyant woman that I go and see, and she told me that in my last lifetime I was a Mohican Indian and I had my brain removed.

Peter Gabriel 1974 •1013

The stars are matter, we're matter, but it doesn't matter.

Captain Beefheart 1971 •1014

I was outside the canopy of the earth, past the planets and into the stars, juiced up by some cosmic petrol-pump attendant. Julian Cope •1015

Although I can see this world and a horrible situation, I also have a belief in other worlds. I'm just a believer of the fairies, I just feel the fairies in my stomach... I communicate with the fairies instinctively, I just hear things.

Tori Amos 1992 •1016

22

One man caught on a barbed wire fence.
One man he resist.
One man washed on an empty beach.
One man betrayed with a kiss.
In the name of love.
What more in the name of love?
U2 *Pride (In The Name of Love)* (1984)
from the album *Unforgettable Fire* •1017

(PRIDE
(IN THE
NAME OF
LOVE))

They looked to me like they would be a great
rock band. I've only had to be right once.
Paul McGuinness manager of U2 •1018

We used to look at bands who could play better
and look better, and we used to say, 'They have
everything but it. We had nothing but it.' Bono •1019

Rock 'n' roll is ridiculous. It's absurd. In the
past, U2 was trying to duck that. Now we're
wrapping our arms around it and giving it a
great big kiss. Bono •1020

The rhythm section consists of
four people. The Edge is all four.
BB King on working with U2 •1021

U2 is an original species... there are colours
and feelings and emotional terrain that we
occupy that is ours and ours alone. Bono •1022

What's special about U2 is the music, not the musician. I and the others are just ordinary people and our trade is to make music. Someone else's is to build houses or work in a factory or teach. We're just getting to grips with our trade as songwriters. Bono •1023

We broke up the band after *War*. We literally broke up the band and formed another band with the same name and the same members. Bono •1024

U2 are simple though, aren't they? I mean, I've said it before and I'll say it again, they're definitely simple. My window cleaner's got more to say than that cunt, let's face it. Mark E. Smith 1990 •1025

When you're mega you can afford an independence that a lot of those so-called Indie bands can't. Bono •1026

I remember the pressures it was made under. I remember writing lyrics on the microphone and at £50 an hour that's quite a pressure. Lillywhite was pacing up and down in the studio... he coped really well. Bono on making *October* •1027

Being a rock star is like having a sex change. People stare at you, follow you down the street shouting comments, they hustle you and touch you up. I now know what it must feel like to be a woman. Bono 1992 •1028

I never went to college, I've slept in some strange places, but the library wasn't one of them. I studied rock and roll and I grew up in Dublin in the 70s, music was an alarm bell for me, it woke me up to the world.

`Bono` on receiving an honorary doctorate from the University of Pennysylvania •1029

My heroes are all alive. I never have worshipped at that altar of burnt-out youth.

`Bono` •1030

When you sing, you make people vulnerable to change in their lives. You make yourself vulnerable to change in your life. But in the end, you've got to become the change you want to see in the world. `Bono` •1031

In the Eighties we have to say that rock 'n' roll went to work for the corporation, and got up at six o'clock in the morning. `Bono` 1988 •1032

It's not enough to rage against the lie... you've got to replace it with the truth.

`Bono` •1033

I'm not in a position to be seen as a spokesman for a generation. I mean, how can you be a spokesman of a generation if you've nothing to say, other than 'Help!'

`Bono` attr •1034

I do see myself as a modern prophet, it's true. Some people can't handle that.

`Bono` attr •1035

Eight million people die every year for the price of going out with your friends to the movies and buying an ice cream. Literally for about $30 a head per year, you could save 8 million lives. Isn't that extraordinary? Preventable disease – not calamity, not famine, nothing like that. Preventable disease – just for the lack of medicines. That is cheap, that is a bargain.

Bono solves the world's problems •1036

What a city, what a night, what a crowd, what a bomb, what a mistake, what a wanker you have for a President.

Bono acceptance speech at the MTV Europe Music Awards, referring to French nuclear testing in Pacific, 1996 •1038

Now let me tell you something, I've had enough of Irish Americans who haven't been back to their country, in 20 or 30 odd years, come up to me and talk about the Resistance, the Revolution back home, and the glory of the Revolution, and the glory of dying for the Revolution. Fuck the Revolution! They don't talk about the glory of killing for the Revolution.

What's the glory, in taking a man from his bed and gunning him down in front of his wife and his children? Where's the glory in that? Where's the glory, in bombing a Remembrance Day parade of old age pensioners, the medals taken out and polished up for the day, where's the glory in that? To leave them dying, or crippled for life, or dead, under the rubble of the Revolution that the majority of the people in my country, don't want! Say no more! No more! No more! Wipe your tears away!

Bono as U2 prepare to play *Sunday Bloody Sunday* live •1037

I actually didn't want him on the stage, 'cause his haircut at the time was so appalling.

Geldof on Bono at Live Aid •1039

He's a poet. He's a philosopher. And last night, I think I saw him walking on water.

Mick Jagger on Bono, 1999 •1040

Bono would love to be six foot tall and thin and good-looking. But he's not. He reminds me of a sodding mountain goat.

Ian McCulloch •1041

After meeting Bono, it made me want to give up being in a rock and roll band.

Dave Grohl of Nirvana, 1992 •1042

**I am not frightened of dying,
Anytime will do, I don't mind.**

Quoted at the beginning of
Great Gig In The Sky, from
Pink Floyd's *Dark Side
of the Moon,* (1973) The voice
is that of Gerry, the doorman
at the Abbey Road Studios
where Floyd were recording.

•1043

GREAT GIG IN THE SKY

23

It's funny the way most people love the dead. Once you are dead, you are made for life. A prescient Jimi Hendrix •1044

Now here is a young cat, extremely talented. For years, all the Negroes who'd made it into the white market made it through servility, like Fats Domino, a lovable, jolly fat image. Now here's this cat, you know – 'I am a super spade man, I am like black and tough. And I will fuck you and rape you and do you in, and I'm bad-assed and weird.' Mike Bloomfield on Jimi Hendrix •1045

If I seem free, it's because I'm always running.

Jimi Hendrix •1046

I'm the one that's got to die when it's time for me to die, so let me live my life the way I want to.

Jimi Hendrix •1047

I don't think Jimi committed suicide in the conventional way. He just decided to exit when he wanted to. Eric Burdon on Hendrix' suicide •1048

When they told me he was dead I felt fucking angry. I felt, shit, he let me down. I felt betrayed even though it wasn't a conscious decision for him to die. I felt like the loneliest person on earth. Eric Clapton on the death of Jimi Hendrix •1049

People, whether they know it or not, like their blues singers miserable. They like their blues singers to die afterwards.

Janis Joplin •1050

Jim Morrison was possessed by a vision, by a madness, by a rage to live, by an all-consuming fire to make art. Ray Manzarek •1051

**I am the lizard king.
I can do anything.**
Jim Morrison •1052

**I was and am a free spirit.
I wanted to gather information
and experience everything! To
get out and really live, not just
hang around the house and dream.**

Marc Bolan •1053

I'm very erratic but that's part of art and I consider myself to be an artist, and I don't feel any compunction to be professional if I don't feel like it, or play if I don't want to.

Marc Bolan 1974 •1054

Don't worry, it's not loaded.

Last words of Chicago's `Terry Kath` before shooting himself in 1978 •1055

We live in a country where John Lennon takes six bullets to the chest and Yoko Ono is standing next to him – no fucking bullet. Explain that to me.

`Denis Leary` American comedian •1056

Rob: Liking both Marvin Gaye and Art Garfunkel is like supporting both the Israelis and the Palestinians.
Laura: No, it's really not, Rob. You know why? Because Marvin Gaye and Art Garfunkel make pop records.
Rob: Made. Made. Marvin Gaye is dead. His father shot him.

`John Cusack` (Rob) and `Iben Hjejle` (Laura) in *High Fidelity* (2000) •1057

I've only been in love with a beer bottle and a mirror.

`Sid Vicious` *Sounds*, 1976 •1058

Sid Vicious was just a mindless twerp. I didn't find anything at all romantic about him – or even interesting.

`David Bowie` circa 1983 •1059

Me live in the world but I'm not of the world.

Bob Marley •1060

**And it seems to me you lived your life
Like a candle in the wind.**
Elton John *Candle In The Wind*
(with Bernie Taupin), (1973) from the album
Goodbye Yellow Brick Road. A song about
the fragile life of Marilyn Monroe •1061

**I was the first to know that Ian had died.
It was like a void, like someone had taken
a bridge out from under us.** Peter Hook on the
death of Ian Curtis •1062

You don't have cancer, it has you.

Ian Dury the week he died, April 2000 •1063

The worst crime is faking it.

Kurt Cobain •1064

If you die you're completely happy and your soul somewhere lives on. I'm not afraid of dying. Total peace after death, becoming someone else is the best hope I've got. Kurt Cobain •1065

Thank you all from the pit of my burning, nauseous stomach for your letters and concerns during the last years. I'm too much of an erratic, moody person, and I don't have the passion anymore.

from Kurt Cobain's suicide note, 1994 •1066

My my, hey hey
Rock and roll is here to stay.
Better to burn out
Than to fade away
My my, hey hey.

Neil Young *My My, Hey Hey (Out of the Blue),* (1979) from the album *Rust Never Sleeps.* Quoted on Kurt Cobain's suicide note •1067

I just wish Eddie Vedder would get on with it and kill himself.

Noel Gallagher of Oasis, 1996 •1068

You're nobody til somebody kills you.

Notorious B.I.G. *You're Nobody,* (1997) from the album *Life After Death* •1069

It always happens, all the niggaz that change the world die, they don't get to die like regular people, they die violently.

Tupac Shakur •1070

I believe that everything that you do bad comes back to you. So everything that I do that's bad, I'm going to suffer from it. But in my mind, I believe what I'm doing is right. So I feel like I'm going to heaven. Tupac Shakur •1071

Gonna be some sweet sounds
Coming down on the nightshift.

The Commodores *Nightshift,* (1985)
from the album *Nightshift.* A song
dedicated to dead heroes •1072

We were supposed to be the alt-country Nirvana.
I guess I was supposed to hang myself with
a banjo string. Ryan Adams of Whiskeytown, 2000 •1073

Poets usually have very unhappy endings. Look at Keats' life. Look at Jim Morrison, if you want to call him a poet. Look at him. Although some people say that he really is in the Andes. Bob Dylan 1991 •1074

Every year is getting shorter, never seem to find the time,
Plans that either come to naught or half a page of scribbled lines.
Hanging on in a quiet desperation is the English way,
The time is gone, the song is over, thought I'd something more to say.

Pink Floyd *Time* (1973) from the album *Dark Side Of The Moon* •1075

THANKS TO

Palmer, Myles (ed.)
Small Talk, Big Names
(Edinburgh: Mainstream Publishing, 1993)

Dellio, Phil & Woods, Scott (ed.)
Quotable Pop: Five Decades of Blah Blah Blah
(Toronto: Quotable Books, 2001)

Luerssen, John D. (ed.)
Mouthing Off: A Dictionary of Rock & Roll Quotes
(New York: The Telegraph Company, 2002)

The Times Book of Quotations
(Glasgow: Times Books, 2000)

Andrews, Robert (ed.)
The New Penguin Dictionary of Modern Quotations
(London: Penguin, 2003)

**The biggest source of reference were the
music magazines, online and in paper form;**
Melody Maker, Mojo, NME, Q, Rolling Stone, Uncut, Word

and thanks to *365sing.com* **for lyric checking**